CW01390813

A TIME TRAVELLER'S Field Notes
AND
OBSERVATIONS
OF
DINOSAURS

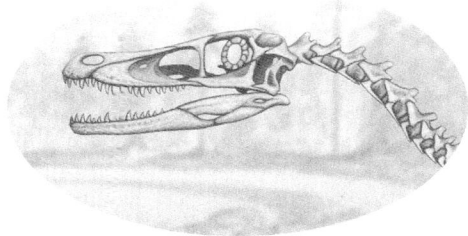

by H. Gray

Quest

This edition published in Great Britain in 2008 by Quest, an imprint of Top That! Publishing plc, Marine House, Tide Mill Way, Woodbridge, Suffolk IP12 1AP, UK
www.topthatpublishing.com

0 2 4 6 8 9 7 5 3 1

All rights reserved. No part of this publication may be reproduced, stored in a retrieval system, or transmitted in any form or by any means, electronic, mechanical, photocopying, recording or otherwise, without the prior written permission of the publisher. Neither this book nor any part nor any of the illustrations, photographs or reproductions contained in it shall be sold or disposed of otherwise than as a complete book, and any unauthorised sale of such part illustration, photograph or reproduction shall be deemed to be a breach of the publisher's copyright.

ISBN 978-1-84666-621-6

A catalogue record for this book is available from the British Library
Printed and bound in China

This is a work of fiction. Names, characters, places, incidents and dialogues are products of the author's imagination or are used fictitiously. Any resemblance to actual people, living or dead, events or locales is entirely coincidental.

Creative Director – Simon Couchman. Editorial Director – Daniel Graham. Art Editor – Matt Denny.
Written by Gordon Volke. Prehistoric illustrations by Robert Nicholls. Character illustrations by Neil Reed.

A TIME TRAVELLER'S
Field Notes
AND
OBSERVATIONS
OF
DINOSAURS

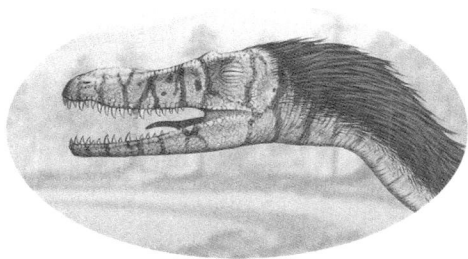

by H. Gray

Quest

Summertime

August 2nd, 1915

The Old Vicarage, Little Waltham.

What a wonderful summer we are having this year! Since early May, the sun has shone from a cloudless blue sky, making the hills and fields around the village shimmer like a mirage. Now we have reached August, the days are so hot that the dust from the roads rises up like smoke and the horses queue for a drink from the water trough in the high street. Even old Mr Givens, who runs the village shop, has taken off his jacket, revealing a splendid pair of bright red braces. It has never been known!

Alas! If only I could enjoy this summer idyll. With Father away at The War, a cloud hangs over me all the time. I worry that he is having a terrible time in the trenches. I worry even more that he won't come back. I know he is a chaplain and not a soldier, but he is still at the mercy of all those dreadful shells and bullets, and he would not think twice about risking his life to help someone in trouble. Oh, why must men fight wars?

Dear Father! I miss him so much. He is the gentlest and kindest man in the whole wide world.

Our old summer house and
the rickety old shed behind.

Anyway, here I am as usual in the summer house at the bottom
of our garden. This is where Father conducts his scientific
experiments and where I am continuing his work while he is away.
I love knowledge. It sustains me like the air that I breathe. I
want to know everything I can about this wonderful world of ours.

My sketch of Mr Givens' shop. It is quite an Aladdin's Cave. You can buy anything in there, from
shoelaces to sacks of coal. Mrs Givens is nice, too. She has two red cheeks like shiny apples and always
calls you 'dearie.'

GIVENS.

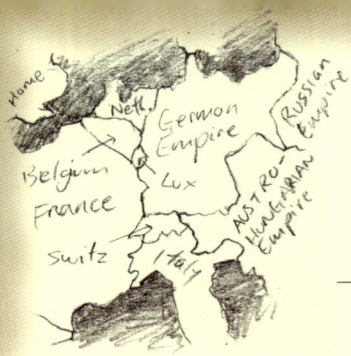

A Discovery

A strange machine is hidden in the shed.

The shed

Mama worries that I spend so much time in the summer house. She thinks I am too much on my own. I keep telling her that I am perfectly happy, but this did not stop her finding me a friend in the shape of a penfriend in Switzerland. I wrote to this girl, telling her that I was fourteen and lived in a village called Little Waltham. I have twin sisters, Lydia and Kate, who are sixteen, and a younger brother, Tom, who is ten. I added that I love science and drawing. The girl did not write back. Obviously, she found me too boring.

This is Kate

Lydia and Kate with Mama.

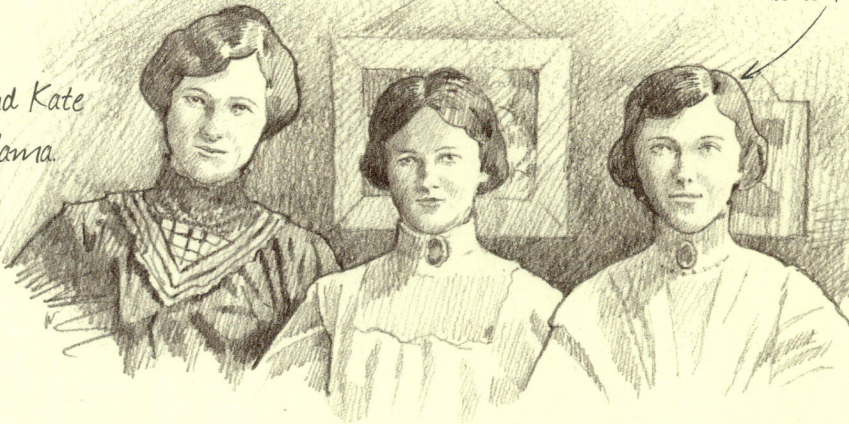

Lydia and Kate think I am boring. They say so to my face. They call me a 'plain little thing' and a 'bookworm'. Tom is equally rude. He calls me a 'horrid bore' because I do not play with him as much as I used to. I do not care. I find their company equally dull. The twins are only concerned about the latest fashions and how they look, while Tom has to be on the go all the time and needs constant entertaining. I tire of my siblings' company as quickly as they tire of mine.

The fields, behind the house, that Tom and I used to play on.

I do have one good friend, however, and that is you, dear Diary! I can tell you all my thoughts and feelings … and my secrets. I know you will not divulge anything to anybody, as long as I keep you away from prying eyes. So, I will tell you something that I would not dream of telling anyone else. There is a strange machine hidden in the shed behind the summer house! On a shelf beside it, there is an old biscuit tin containing a huge crystal that pulsates with a menacing bright green light.

Although the machine is covered in a thick layer of dust and grime, there is an obvious recessed compartment that perfectly matches the shape of the crystal. What happens when the two are put together, I cannot imagine … but I mean to find out!

This is the crystal. Father never mentioned it, but I have since read some notes he kept hidden in the shed and learned how it came into his possession. He was using his telescope late one night when he saw a strange green light fall to earth. Next day, he went to investigate and found this beautiful crystal pulsating in the grass. I believe it could be from another world.

What will happen when the strange machine and the crystal are reunited?

The Riddle

August 4th, 1915

All knowledge, ever known and yet to be known, is only a switch away.

I gave in this morning and went out into the fields with Tom. We pretended to be explorers, finding our way around a strange land full of terrible dangers. I must confess, I enjoyed myself enormously – even though I am supposed to have grown out of such games. We came home at the end of the morning with scraped knees and faces stained by the juice of wild blackberries, just like we did years ago. Good job Mama did not see me. She would have said it was not ladylike!

Tom wanted me to go out with him again this afternoon, but I said 'no' this time. My mind was running on more important things. If only I could make sense of the mathematical formulae in Father's hidden notes! And what did he mean when he wrote this:

'It is built and now I must put theory into action. All knowledge, ever known and yet to be known, is only a switch away.'

I shall find out this afternoon. At luncheon, Mama announced that she was taking Lydia and Kate to the dressmaker's and Tom has now arranged to visit his friend, Daniel.

Part of the control console in the cockpit of Father's machine.

At three o'clock, I went into the shed and put the crystal in its allotted space on Father's strange machine. The following account is a record of the unbelievable events that occurred in the ensuing hours:

3.35pm Nothing at all happened! No, that is not correct — one small set of number dials started spinning. I pressed a switch at the side of the dials which abruptly stopped the mechanism. As the dials jerked to a halt, the number '605' lined up beside a pointer labelled 'MYA'.

3.42pm The whole machine started to shake. I could feel it lifting off the ground and wondered where I was going. My head was in a spin. I was scared and nauseous.

3.45pm I felt a heavy BUMP, and the noise and confusion was replaced by a strange and eerie silence. It appeared that my short journey was over. I spent the next couple of minutes mustering the necessary courage to open the door.

3.50pm After much fidgeting and clock watching I opened the door. This decision changed my life completely and forever in an instant!

The Time Machine

The Dawn of Time

'MYA' stands for Millions of Years Ago!

Ah! What a scene lay before my eyes! At first I thought I was on another planet, somewhere out in space.

Then, it struck me! The letters 'MYA' stand for 'Millions of Years Ago'. If my theory is correct, then I had miraculously travelled back 605 million years, to a time when the Earth was still forming. I have since learnt that this era of time is referred to as the Precambrian Period.

I decided to fetch my sketch pad and record everything that I saw. The pictures were coloured later, when I had more time.

This dramatic panorama was my first impression of the Precambrian Period.

The sea was a beautiful shade of emerald green.

The shore was littered with strange mushroom-shaped rocks.

The moon seemed far larger
than at home.

The landscape
was dominated
by enormous
active volcanoes.

Dawn of Time

The Precambrian Period

Take notes. Collect samples. Be a scientist!

My head told me to go home right away and be safe. But my heart kept saying:

'You are visiting the dawn of time! You are seeing things that nobody has ever seen before. Make the most of it! Go outside and look around. Take notes. Collect samples. Be a scientist!' I had to obey my heart!

As soon as I stepped outside, I found it hard to get my breath. The air was very thin, like being on the top of a high mountain. With so little oxygen around, I could not exert myself too much or I might have fainted.

I came across some loose stones by the sea. They were covered in green slime. I picked a few up and took them back with me for analysis.

The green slime on the rock was algae, one of the earliest forms of life. The water around it was a strange dark green colour. I have since found out that this was due to the chemicals and minerals dissolved in it.

Rock sample

Suddenly, what had been an exciting adventure turned into a potential disaster! A loud rumbling sound made me look in the direction of the horizon. Then I saw a tidal wave, hundreds of feet high, hurtling towards me at the speed of an express steam train. I was frozen with fear. Gulping as much precious oxygen into my lungs as I could, I raced back towards my time machine!

I made it with just seconds to spare. The little craft rocked as the first wave of water swirled around its legs. I panicked, not knowing what to do next. Then I applied some logic and set the dial to 1915 AD. I hoped it would take me back to my own time.

It worked! The crystal glowed again, followed by the same violent shaking and a euphoric feeling of lift-off.

Precambrian tidal wave.

Field notes and observations: I painted this picture of the tidal wave in the peace and safety of my beloved shed. I have since discovered that these gigantic tidal waves were caused by the Moon being so much closer to the Earth than it is today. The roar as this wall of water approached was truly terrifying.

My tent

A New Friend

August 4th, 1915

Food provisions:
Chocolate, Biscuits (savoury),
Dried fruit, Biscuits (sweet),
Tinned meat, tinned beans &
tinned soup (tomato!).

Father's time machine gives me unique access to the past.

Evening If I did not have the samples of rock in my possession, I would have thought this whole thing was a dream. Stranger still, the clock in the shed still showed forty two minutes past three when I returned, even though I had been gone for just under three hours. Obviously, time-travelling time is different from real time. So, my family will never miss me, even though I could be gone for days or weeks.

I wish I could tell Father of my adventure … Oh, foolish me! I have been so blind! He did not mean to keep this marvellous machine hidden. He meant for me to discover it and use it because he is unable to! Very well then! I shall honour his wish.

My first journey has taught me some valuable lessons. In future, I must make sure I do these important things –

Kit items

Tent, lamp & fuel √

water canteen √

cooking pot √

penknife √

tin opener √

compass √

matches & tinder box √

rope √

mallet √

1. Be prepared for visiting a strange environment. I shall need food, water, camping equipment and many other items essential for survival.

IMPORTANT!
Replenish art materials!

2. Keep a record of everything I see. Father's invention gives me unique access to the past. I will be experiencing history first-hand. I must preserve all my findings in the form of notes, sketches and paintings so I can discuss them with Father when he returns.

3. Make sure I always get back safely!

I am sorry, dear Diary. Your days are over. From now on, you are going to be known as my Journal!

August 5th, 1915

Morning I have been busy preparing for my first proper journey into the past and I have made some big decisions …

Mr Givens was a bit suspicious when I started buying lots of food and supplies, so I told him I was going camping with some friends. His wife came to my rescue, saying:

'If these newfangled Boy Scouts can go to camp, Herbert, so can the girls. Isn't that right, dearie?'

To start with, I was not sure where to go. There are so many exciting times and places to explore. Once again, though, dearest Father has made up my mind for me. He is passionate about dinosaurs and keeps a book up to date with the latest discoveries. So, I intend to return to prehistory, starting my journey in the Triassic Period about 230 million years ago. This is the first great age of the dinosaurs and there should be plenty to see.

Botheration! Mama has just called down the garden to say that Aunt Harriet and Cousin Millicent have come to call. That is the last thing I want to happen at the moment – a visit from my nosy cousin and her snobbish mother!

Nosy Cousin Millicent.

Prehistory Preparations
August 5th, 1915

At all times everything must be kept secret!

Evening **W**hy do grown-ups always assume that children will get on with each other just because they are the same age? Millicent only had to express a desire to see my scientific studies for Mama to pack us straight off to the summer house together.

Hoping my cousin would soon lose interest, I left her to wander around the laboratory area on her own. I knew she did not really care a fig about what I was doing. But did she grow bored? Not at all! She made a beeline straight for the shed door!

'What's in there?' she asked.

'Nothing,' I replied.

'You won't mind showing me, then!' she demanded.

It took a long and tiring battle of wills to convince Millicent that there was nothing of any import behind that locked door. I am not even sure that I succeeded, for I caught her a little while later, standing on tiptoe, trying to peep through the grimy windows. She suspects there is a secret hidden in there – and she is right. But she must never, ever, find out what it is!

Our guests left after tea. At least I have learned another golden rule from my hateful cousin's visit –

4. At all times, everything must be kept secret!

First thing tomorrow morning, before everyone is up, I shall depart on my journey. I have everything I need stowed away in the hold of the time machine. Now I must try to get some sleep. Goodnight, dear Journal. Our adventure begins at first light.

My Journey To
THE TRIASSIC PERIOD

The Triassic Period was 245-208 Million Years Ago

Triassic Terror

Day 1 in the Triassic Period

230 million years ago!

Just after sunrise I am standing in a forest clearing 230 million years ago and I am surrounded by giant seed-ferns that reach over my head like huge hands! Everywhere in the distance I can see conifer trees. The cones they produce are enormous. It is like looking at a Scottish hillside through a giant magnifying glass!

Giant ferns and conifers grow in such abundance here.

Mid-morning Something came crashing through the undergrowth. It sounded big, so I got out of its way by climbing up a tree. What a powerful-looking beast it was! It had a massive head of about three feet long and jaws full of very sharp teeth. It was shaped a bit like a crocodile, but much taller and heavier. I made a mental note to look it up in Father's book later on.

Erythrosuchus

Father's book contains a reference for every prehistoric creature. The one I encountered earlier today is an Erythrosuchus. The name is pronounced 'Erry-throw-soo-chus' and means 'red crocodile'.

Erythrosuchus isn't a dinosaur but an archosaur relative. It is one of the foremost predators of the time.

I thought the creature had gone and was just getting down from my perch in the tree when it spotted me and came back to investigate. It was obviously a meat-eating predator … and a hungry one at that. It threw its huge bulk against the tree in an attempt to shake me down. I had to hold on with both hands until my knuckles were white.

My ordeal lasted about half an hour. After that, the monster lost interest and moved on. I must be very careful. Otherwise, I will end up as prey!

The creature possessed teeth like steak knives!

IMPORTANT NOTE:

I was inaccurate earlier when I described the Erythrosuchus as having a head about three feet long. Such Imperial measures are acceptable for everyday conversation, but not for a scientific journal like mine. I should have said 'one metre long'. From now on, I shall use the decimal measures

Day 1 in the Triassic Period (continued)

Afternoon I have discovered a low headland overlooking some extensive marshes. It looks a perfect place to pitch my tent. Tonight, I shall hide the time machine with some bracken and camp there.

Earlier this afternoon, I saw a strange creature swimming towards me through the shallows. It looked like something from an ancient Celtic myth. It had an incredibly long neck, which it kept dipping into the water. Every time it did so, scores of small fish simultaneously breached the surface in what appeared to be an attempt to escape. Judging by the abundance of fish bones on the shoreline, I think it is safe to assume that this creature was feeding on the fish.

I am pleased with this painting of the creature coming towards me out of the marshes. It captures the atmosphere of the moment.

I found lots of fish bones on the shoreline.

As it lumbered ashore I could see that its neck was longer than both its body and tail together. It seemed a wonder that the animal did not keep toppling over!

Then something frightened the creature away. No matter! I had a good look at it. I shall spend what is left of the day drawing and painting what I saw. Then at least I will have a proper record for my journal.

Tanystropheus

This is what the creature looked like when it was out of the water. Is it not all out of proportion? I still fail to understand how it managed to keep its balance.

According to Father's book, I was looking at a Tanystropheus ('Tan-ee-strow-fee-us' which means 'long, narrow bones'). It is not a dinosaur. It is an archosaur that spends part of its time in the water and part of its time on land. That is the only information entered. Although its bones were first discovered sixty years ago, in 1855, nothing very much seems to be known about it. Maybe I can add to science's knowledge of this creature through observing it in the wild?

Here is a sketch of the head. It has a long snout and the teeth fit together very tightly Any fish that the creature catches has no chance of wriggling away!

Tanystropheus close-up

My last entry for today

I am frightened! Since sunset, I have had the feeling that I am being watched. There is a constant rustling in the bushes surrounding my campsite and I hear the occasional snort and growl. It could be my imagination, but I fear I'm being stalked by a predator.

Escape Mechanism
Day 2 in the Triassic Period

'Nature is red in tooth and claw' – Alfred Tennyson.

Mid-morning **M**y hand is shaking so much, I can barely write. I have just experienced a terror worse than any nightmare.

I was awoken just after first light by a foul stench. Opening my eyes, I found my tent tossed aside and the ugly, snarling face of the Erythrosuchus breathing right into mine!

I screamed so loudly that my throat is still hoarse. Obviously, the beast had never heard such a high-pitched sound before. It recoiled for a moment and that gave me time to escape. I scrambled up some nearby rocks faster than a squirrel running up a tree!

To my surprise, the Erythrosuchus did not pursue me. The Tanystropheus I saw yesterday came splashing past through some shallow water, chasing a small animal. Spotting it, the Erythrosuchus turned aside with a stomach-churning roar and thundered after it. I watched the long-necked reptile struggle through the clinging vegetation, trying to reach the safety of the open water.

All my life, I have endeavoured to have a scientific attitude and view everything without emotion, so I know that a predator should never be judged for the way in which it finds its food. After all, my favourite poet, Tennyson, said, 'Nature is red in tooth and claw'. And yet, having nearly been the victim of this horrible killer, I could not help being on the side of the Tanystropheus. I found myself standing up and yelling:

'Go on! Go on! Keep going!'

My cries were to no avail. The Erythrosuchus opened its terrible jaws and closed in for the kill.

Then an amazing thing happened! As the predator's teeth took hold of the Tanystropheus' tail, it broke off! At first, I thought this was some terrible wound, but then I realised that it was supposed to happen. It is an escape mechanism! Some modern-day lizards still use the same device.

With a roar of fury, the attacker swallowed his tiny morsel while the would-be victim made his getaway into deep water. How I cheered – silently, of course, in case the hunter turned his attention back to me! Then it was all over. The Tanystropheus disappeared under the waves. The Erythrosuchus crashed off in search of another meal. And I was left realising that I had witnessed something of major importance. Tanystropheus sheds its tail as a defence mechanism. My wish has come true. I have added something to our knowledge of prehistoric creatures!

The ferocious Erythrosuchus attack as I witnessed it this morning.

Albert

Day 6 in the Triassic Period

Close-up of Coelophysis' blade-like teeth.

I have found a friend to keep me company.

Coelophysis have small forelimbs with grasping hands.

First light This is a lonely and desolate place. I have only my own company night and day and my work has become dangerous and unpredictable. Maybe all this rain has something to do with my misery? It has not stopped for the past three days. If it continues much longer, I shall have to strike camp and move to higher ground to avoid becoming waterlogged.

Mid-morning What a surprise! I have found a friend to keep me company. It is a small dinosaur that walks on its hind legs. He hopped into my clearing looking lost and hungry so I fed him some scraps. Now he will not go away. He is not exactly tame – he is a sharp-toothed carnivore from whom I keep a respectful distance – but there is definitely a bond between us. I have named him Albert.

Name : Coelophysis
Pronunciation : 'See-low-fie-iss'
Meaning of name : 'hollow form'

Albert

The long tail is used like a rudder to help the animal change direction.

Description in Father's book: A lightly-built dinosaur about one metre tall and two to three metres in length. It moves on two powerful legs and has two smaller forelimbs. Evidence suggests that it lived in a pack.

Dusk Albert was restless and excited this afternoon and made frequent forays out of the camp. I followed him along a steep, well-beaten track and it proved to be my salvation. The ground was much drier higher up and so I decided to pitch a new camp on a small plateau halfway up the hill.

I soon learned what was agitating Albert. He had found his pack again! He must have been separated from them when he met me, but quickly went off to join them when he heard them squabbling and fighting over a kill.

As I watched Albert tuck into his feast a dark shadow passed over my head. Looking up, I saw a flying reptile with a wingspan of at least a metre. I did not need Father's book to tell me this was a pterosaur (pronounced 'teh-row-sore', meaning 'winged lizard').

It flew across to a lake in the distance and started skimming the surface, hunting for fish. It will make a splendid picture. It does not look like a living animal. It looks more like one of those new flying machines, called aeroplanes, that have been taking to the skies in recent years.

A pack of Coelophysis feasts on the remains of a kill as a pterosaur flies overhead.

Dark Skies

Day 7 in the Triassic Period

Today the heavens opened!

Morning The storm clouds are gathering again, blacker than ever. My time on this hilltop is limited. I must make the most of it by taking notes and sketching the amazing creatures that I can see.

Late afternoon A deluge of biblical proportions forced me to stop making field notes and observations. I wrapped my precious journal and art materials in an oilskin bag, to prevent them from getting wet, and tucked the bag inside my coat before taking refuge in a copse further down the hill.

Desmatosuchus

I saw a big armoured dinosaur about five metres long and two metres high. Father's book identifies it as a Desmatosuchus. That is pronounced 'Des-mat-oh-soo-chus' and means 'link crocodile.' It had a huge spike above each shoulder from which a row of spikes ran either side to the tip of its tail.

This beast is a phytosaur (Fie-toh-sore meaning 'plant reptile'). Father's notes state that this name is misleading. Their many teeth and long, snapping jaws clearly show that they are predators.

The one I observed (a Rutiodon) was massive, over four metres long.

Rutiodon

This goliath animal is a plant-eating Plateosaurus (Plat-ee-oh-sore-us, meaning 'flat lizard'). The one I saw was at least ten metres long and must have weighed several tonnes.

Plateosaurus

Washed Away!
Day 9 in the Triassic Period

The unrelenting rain caused a catastrophic mudslide.

It is now two days since the disaster. I must have lain unconscious for one of them, having hit my head on a rock as a cascade of mud and water surged through the copse. It has taken most of today to recover from my ordeal. Only now do I feel well enough to resume my journal. At least that is safe. All I remember is clutching it tight to my chest as I was swept down the hillside by the malevolent torrent.

I have resolved to find my time machine and return to the present as soon as possible … but first I feel compelled to observe and record the extraordinary scene that lies before me.

Poor Albert is dead. All the Coelophysis are dead. They lie in a mangled heap, drowned and broken by the mudslide that caught us all unawares.

Down here, on the beach, lies the partially decomposed carcass of an enormous marine creature – twenty metres long at least. How it comes to be washed up here, I cannot say. Maybe it became stranded in the way that whales still do today?

This is the third day that I have not eaten. I am tempted to join the host of scavengers who are feeding on this unfortunate reptile, but the idea of eating raw meat completely turns my stomach.

Let us hope my time machine remains intact. Otherwise, I shall be like the Shonisaurus – stranded here until I die!

This enormous marine reptile is called a Shonisaurus (pronounced 'Shon-ee-saw-rus' meaning 'Shoshone Mountains reptile'). The dead specimen that I observed was twenty-three metres in length and has four powerful flippers, a dorsal fin and a tail rather like that of a dolphin.

Shonisaurus

Note: Father's book contains an amusing fact. The first Shonisaurus skeleton was discovered by silver miners. They took home some of the heavy, round vertebrae and used them as dinner plates!

Note to self:
Must do proper
repairs when I
get home.

Heading Home

Day 10 in the Triassic Period

I cannot wait to leave the Triassic Period.

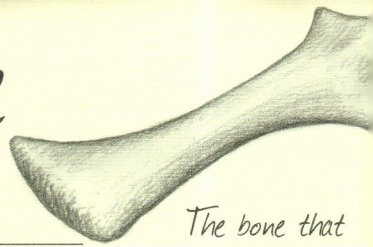

The bone that saved me.

Late morning

My worst fear materialised earlier today when I discovered that my time machine had been damaged by the mudslide. One of the leg struts had broken off rendering it useless. What was worse – something was moving about inside!

Thankfully, the intruder was only a tiny dinosaur, about the size of a rabbit. I opened the door and let it out. I will find out what it is and sketch it when I get home. I can't wait to leave the Triassic … but I still have to mend the broken strut.

Afternoon

I attempted to fix the broken leg with some wood and string taken from the cabin. It did not work. So then I looked around – and the solution was right under my nose! A sturdy dinosaur bone lay on the ground at the edge of the clearing. Jammed in hard, it's a perfect fit and has set the time machine at an upright angle. I am ready to depart at last!

Saltopus

The rabbit-sized dinosaur that had taken up residence in my time machine was a Saltopus (pronounced 'Salt-oh-pus' and meaning 'hopping foot'). It moved on two legs and was a fast runner. It had a five-fingered hand and a long head with lots of very sharp teeth. So it was a carnivore.

Species of insect and flora that I identified, using
Father's book, during my expedition.

Sanmiguelia 'flower' – with large
palm-like leaves.

A fly, Architipula

A thrips beetle

Mushrooms

A pack of Coelophysis run across the
foot of a giant Sequoia redwood tree.

Reptiles of the Triassic Period

A comparative scale study

While the memory of my Triassic adventure is still fresh, I have tried to capture the comparative scale of the magnificent reptiles that I observed. This scientific approach to illustration has proved to be the most challenging thus far.

Tanystropheus – 6.5 m long
(a prolacertiform)

Rutiodon – 4 m long
(a phytosaur)

Desmatosuchus – 5 m long
(an aetosaur)

Important note: m = metres and cm = centimetres.

Eudimorphodon – 1 m wingspan
(a pterosaur)

Shonisaurus – 23 m long
(an ichthyosaur)

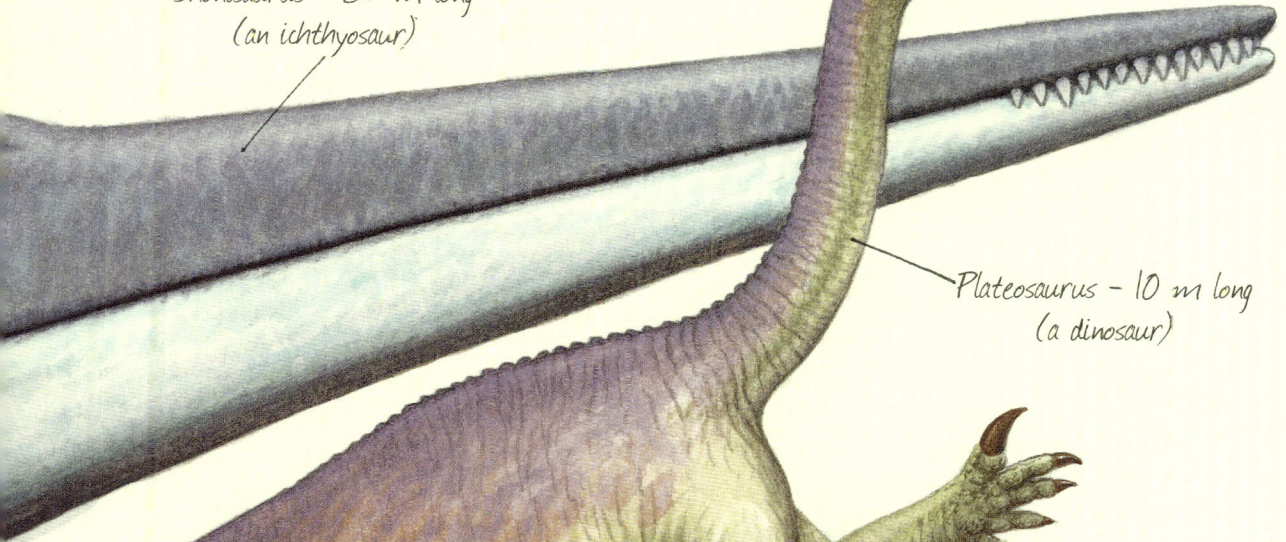

Plateosaurus – 10 m long
(a dinosaur)

Coelophysis – 2 to 3 m long
(a dinosaur)

Erythrosuchus – 5 m long
(an archosauromorph)

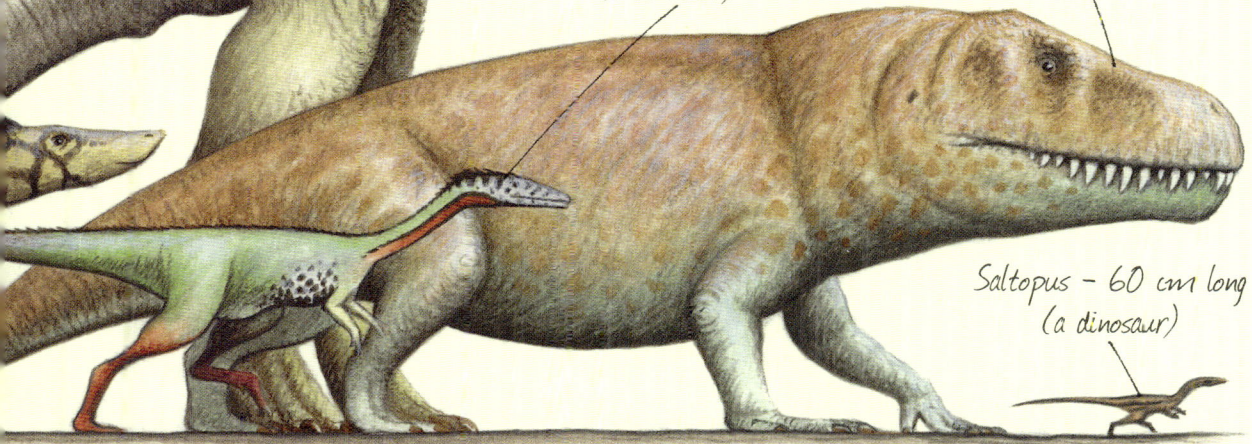

Saltopus – 60 cm long
(a dinosaur)

Bruno

August 8th, 1915

I shall live longer ... because my time spent time-travelling does not count.

The first thing I noticed upon my return to the present was the same strange phenomenon in relation to time. I was away in the Triassic Period for a total of ten days, yet I returned with the summer house clock showing the same moment that I had left. At least everyone is spared the worry of my disappearance, but what will be the effect in the long run? It would seem that I shall live longer than anyone else because my time spent time-travelling does not count.

The big news here is that we have a dog! Mama felt insecure with Father away all the time, so she went to a local farm and bought an unwanted mongrel to act as our guard dog. I think she has made a mistake. Bruno is untrained and unruly. He crashes around the house like a big puppy, knocking things over and upsetting everyone. He looks for love from everyone he meets, so I cannot imagine him being much of a deterrent to a burglar – unless he licks the villain to death!

Mr Givens gave me some very funny looks when I went to replace my lost equipment and replenish my supplies. He even had the audacity to ask me why I needed to purchase so many items again. I declined to answer this time. I fail to see why I should be forced to lie in public because of his nosy questioning. He is only a shopkeeper and should know his place. I shall make a point of going into town next time I need to shop for my trips. Then he will not be able to question what I am doing.

Bruno — the newest member of our family.

This is Bruno. I long to take him under my wing and instil some discipline into him. Dogs are pack animals. They are used to serving and obeying their leader. If a human being fills this role, they know where they are and are happy to serve you to the point of being loyal to the death. But Mama insists upon indulging him like a child, Lydia and Kate treat him like a plaything and Tom delights in his misbehaviour. The poor animal looks so confused. I can see this all ending up in tears. One day, he will disgrace himself and find himself rejected.

I must neglect you for a while now, dearest Journal. I have to prepare for my next time-travelling adventure … to the Jurassic Period.

Bad Behaviour

Poor Bruno has been banished from the house!

The situation with Bruno has turned out just as I predicted ... only in the most amusing of ways!

On Tuesday, the Vicar came to tea. Reverend Thomas, who is standing in for Father in his absence, is perhaps the dullest man who has ever been born. Mother endures his company because she feels it is her duty, but the others go out when he calls and I always beat a hasty retreat to the summer house, citing my studies as an excuse.

Apparently, just as Mama was pouring her finest tea into our best teacups, Bruno came bounding into the room and knocked everything over. Then he proceeded to eat all the fancy cakes that had been thrown onto the floor before ... wait for it ... cocking his leg and relieving himself over the Vicar's shoes! Mama says she has never seen Reverend Thomas leave the house so fast. She pretended to be very cross about the whole business, but I could see a real twinkle in her eyes.

Even so, poor Bruno has been banished from the house. My sisters do not want the same thing happening to their favourite shoes and Tom will only encourage worse behaviour from the dog. So guess who has taken responsibility for him!

Bruno is now based in the summer house. I take him out for walks morning and evening. I feed him regularly. Most important of all, I chastise him gently when he does wrong and praise him warmly when he behaves well. There is much understanding between us already.

I wish Father could have been here to witness today's funny events!

Monday morning I am worried that my secret could have been discovered. It was very hot as I made my final preparations and I foolishly opened the shed window to let in some air. Next minute, Tom's ball bounced inside and he put his head in through the window to ask for it back. I do not know whether he saw the time machine or not. If he did, he probably did not know what it was. However, should he say anything about it, my adventures will be over before they have really begun.

Wednesday evening This is a catastrophe! Just as Bruno was becoming a loyal and obedient dog, he has disappeared! Tom and I have looked everywhere for him and called and called until our throats are hoarse, but there is no sign of him. I hope he comes back soon.

Saturday I wanted to depart this morning, but feel I cannot leave with this crisis unresolved. Tom and I spent all day searching for Bruno, again without success.

Tuesday Still no sign of the dog. I fear he is lost forever.

Private and Confidential

Wednesday, August 25th, 1915

I wish that I had someone to share my adventures with.

Just after midnight   I cannot afford to wait any longer. The school holidays are speeding by and I must leave myself time to recover from any further adventures before I return to school. I shall depart today after a few precious hours in my comfy bed.

Sunrise   Tom has been very upset by the loss of Bruno, so I peeped into his bedroom to check on him before I left. He always looks so sweet when he is asleep, like a little toddler. But he was not in his bed. The sheets were rumpled, so I imagine he was up at first light, scouring the countryside for his lost friend.

I was making some last-minute checks when I heard strange noises coming from the hold of the time machine. First, there were some scraping sounds, followed by a series of muffled grunts and something that resembled a yelp of joy. I listened again, but the noises did not recur. I put them down to my imagination and anxiety just prior to another dangerous journey.

PRIVATE & CONFIDENTIAL:

I don't know whether to go or not. I'm sure this 'middle age' of the dinosaurs will be an extremely exciting place to be, but I feel very much alone in these eerie, non-human places. If only I had someone to talk to and share the experience with. But that is impossible, given that everything must be kept so SECRET.

6 am   I've decided it's time to go!

My Journey To
THE JURASSIC PERIOD

The Jurassic Period was 208-144 Million Years Ago

Jurassic Journey

Day 1 in the Jurassic Period

160 Million Years Ago!

The crystal did not seem to glow as brightly as on my previous trips and it took longer to get here. I hope the crystal is not losing its power. Also, those strange noises did not abate. In fact, they grew louder. I have no idea what could be making them.

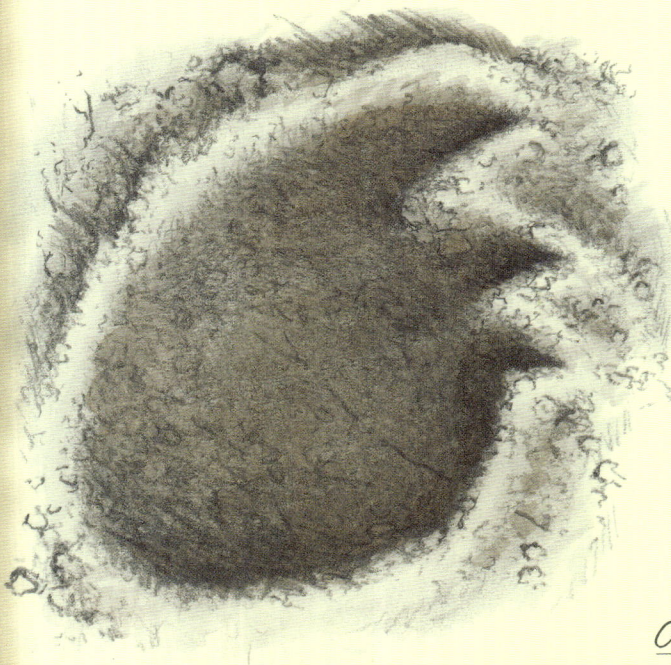

Mystery footprint:
The moment I opened the door of the time machine, I saw something that took my breath away. It was a gigantic footprint that must belong to a huge, plant-eating dinosaur. The question is ... which one? My hope is that it was made by an Amphicoelias (pronounced 'am-fee-see-lee-as' and meaning 'double hollow'), possibly the largest living creature ever to walk on Earth.

Othnielia

A tiny dinosaur tried to befriend me earlier. It was a Othnielia (pronounced 'Oth-nigh-eel-ee-ah' and meaning 'Othniel's dinosaur'). He scuttled along on two legs and looked to me as if he was a herbivore – a plant eater.

Sauropod Spotting
Day 2 in the Jurassic Period

Watching these plant eaters at work is an awesome sight.

I have spent all day observing and drawing three huge plant-eating dinosaurs (scientific name, sauropods). Here they are with a brief summary of Father's notes combined with my own observations …

This is the age of the giant plant-eating dinosaurs. Diplodocus, Brachiosaurus, Apatosaurus, Seismosaurus, Supersaurus and Barosaurus are all around at this time.

Name: Apatosaurus (pronounced 'Ah-pat-oh-saw-rus', meaning 'deceptive lizard')
Observation: This massive creature looks about thirty metres long and must weigh at least twenty tonnes. It is a stocky animal that holds its tail out behind it as it walks along. I saw it use its tail for balance when its head was down, grazing on vegetation. Father's records say that its jaws do not have big grinding teeth for chewing tough plants, so it swallowed stones (proper name gastroliths) to grind up food in its stomach.

Apatosaurus

SPECIAL NOTE:
Sometimes this dinosaur is called a Brontosaurus. The name is incorrect and should not be used.

Watching these plant eaters at work is an awesome sight. They can strip a conifer tree bare in a matter of minutes. One half of the plain before me is a lush, green forest; the other half is a bare wasteland of shredded trees and chewed-off shrubs. Modern elephants devastate whole areas like this. Good job there are miles of fertile open space in the Jurassic!

Name: Barosaurus (pronounced 'Bah-roh-saw-rus', meaning 'heavy lizard').
  Observation: This sauropod has a particularly long neck and tail! The distance
    between the two must be at least twenty-seven metres!

Barosaurus

Name: Brachiosaurus (pronounced 'Brack-ee-oh-saw-rus', meaning 'arm lizard').
Observation: Its front legs are longer than its back ones (rather like a modern giraffe).
Like all the sauropod dinosaurs, it has a very long neck and tail. It has chisel-shaped
teeth, allowing it to bite off leaves and vegetation with ease. I could see that
Brachiosaurus live in family groups or herds. Large numbers of these animals,
combined with their gigantic size, make them hard to attack, even by the most
powerful predators.

A herd of Brachiosaurus

Stowaways

Day 3 in the Jurassic Period

Children accept things as normal that older people find amazing.

I received the shock of my life this morning. I opened the hatch to the hold (which I keep locked for security), and out jumped Bruno! He was full of beans, despite having been cooped up in such a small space for so long. I was just giving him a drink of water when a voice called out to me: 'Can I have some too please, sis?' It was Tom! He had come as a stowaway too!

Later, when my little brother had recovered, he explained that he had heard some faint barking from the region of the summer house. He discovered Bruno trapped in the time machine, which Tom thought was some kind of heating system for the house! He was just in the process of letting the dog out when I arrived and took off. So now they are both here with me.

Tom showed no surprise when I explained about Father's incredible invention. Children of ten are still learning about the world, so they accept things as normal that older people find amazing. He was pleased to be sharing my adventure and, in my heart, I was delighted to have his company, even though he would make short work of my food supplies and hugely increase the chance of something going wrong.

Tom was keen to go dinosaur-spotting, so we left the plateau, where I had set up camp, and scrambled down a rocky slope to the valley below. From here we observed two different animals using the herds of gentle sauropods to their advantage.

I am sure that Bruno was not trapped in the machine for the entire time that he was missing. It is not possible to survive without water for the length of time that he was absent.

Sordes pilosus
in flight.

Name Sordes pilosus (pronounced 'Sore-days pie-low-suss,' meaning 'hairy demon'). Observations: This tiny pterosaur flitted about among these huge dinosaurs like a modern bat, eating insects from their skins.

Name: Dryosaurus (pronounced 'Dry-oh-saw-rus,' meaning 'oak lizard'). Observations: It was a smallish dinosaur that followed the big sauropods for protection. I saw a whole herd keeping pace with the migrating giants, but steering well clear of those pillar-like legs to avoid being trampled on!

Dryosaurus

DUNG NOTE:

One thing that I forgot to mention about the sauropods. Father estimated that a single animal of that size must eat in the region of 400 pounds of vegetation (scientific conversion = 182 kilograms) a day. Given that these animals live in vast herds, and there are several species of them, the amount of dung they create must be truly phenomenal. I hope I never come across any of it!

A Sleepless Night
Day 4 in the Jurassic Period

What have we done?

This Morning

Tom and I feel like characters from 'The Lost World' by Sir Arthur Conan Doyle. It is our favourite book. Father bought me the first edition for my eleventh birthday and I read it to Tom as his bedtime story over and over again. Why do I say this? Because we have just seen an Allosaurus – the main predator in the story!

We had gone out together, leaving Bruno tied up outside the time machine. (The dog wants to play all the time, so he slows us down and gets in the way.) We were halfway up a low hill when we heard a loud snarling noise in the distance. My blood ran cold when the creature came into view. It was an enormously powerful carnivore with the most terrifying set of teeth. I am glad the monster is far away now. I want to avoid another run-in with a hungry meat eater!

Afternoon

What have we done? We have just returned to the time machine, and Bruno has gone! All that remains is a length of chewed-up rope. Tom reckons the Allosaurus has taken him. Poor Bruno! My eyes are full of tears as I write. What a terrible, terrible fate!

Day 5

Tom and I were so upset, we did not speak to each other for the rest of yesterday afternoon. We did not sleep well, either, and have spent all of today moping around our camp. Leaving Bruno was one of the biggest mistakes I have ever made in my life!

The Allosaurus has two blunt horns on his head, just above the eyes.

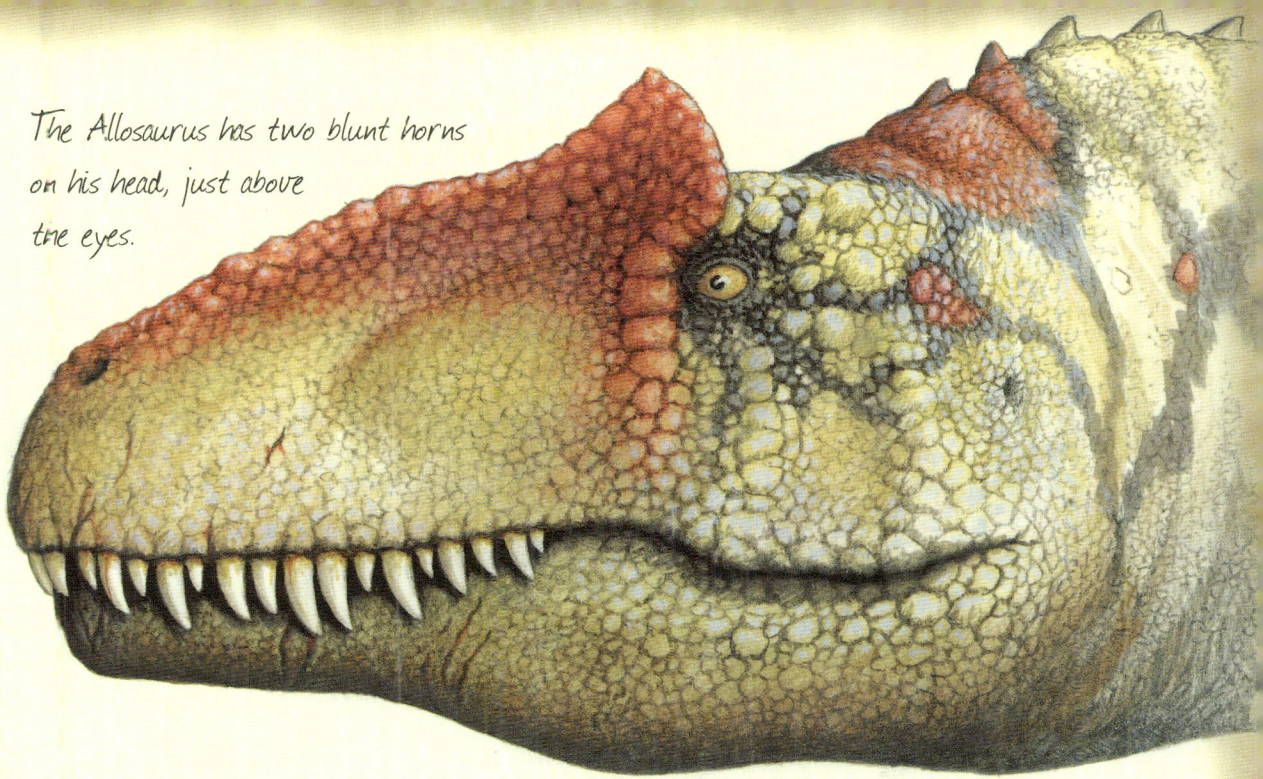

Name: <u>Allosaurus</u> (pronounced 'Al-low-sore-us', meaning 'strange lizard').
Observations: Appears to be the most common predator around at this time.
The specimen I encountered walked on its two hind legs and had a huge, thick skull balanced by a long, heavy tail.

<u>Allosaurus in pursuit of prey.</u>

The Allosaurus has three massive claws on its forelegs. They remind me of the talons of an eagle, only ten times larger!

A Lucky Escape!

Day 6 in the Jurassic Period

Am I getting closer to Father's special dinosaur?

Morning The sun was rising and I was sitting on a rock, weeping quietly over the loss of Bruno, when I became aware of a snorting noise right behind me. I spun around and found myself looking right into the terrifying face of the Allosaurus! Despite its enormous size and bulk, the monster had crept up right behind me without my knowing. I jumped up and ran for my life!

Roaring furiously, the killer came after me. I imagined, by dodging and swerving, I might be able to avoid those cruel teeth and talons – at least until my breath ran out. But I did not bank on finding myself right at the edge of a precipice! I had no option but to jump! I fell through some trees, banging my head on the branches, and that is the last thing I remember.

I came round, feeling pain in almost every part of my body. Something soft had broken my fall. As I felt and smelt it a ghastly realisation dawned on me. I had landed on a gigantic mound of sauropod droppings!

Sliding down to the ground was the most disgusting thing I have ever done in my life. I became covered in foul-smelling dung. Choking and retching, I stumbled away from the mountainous pile and was repeatedly sick.

When I recovered, I noticed many more of the gigantic footprints I had seen on my arrival. Maybe these are Amphicoelias droppings! Am I getting closer to Father's special dinosaur? If so, my revolting adventure will be worthwhile.

Tom was very relieved to see me as I stumbled back to camp. 'PHEW! You stink!' he said, recoiling from giving me a hug. I went and had a (ice-cold) wash under a nearby waterfall and put on some clean clothes. Then Tom made me relate my 'dung adventure' ten times in a row. It makes him cry with laughter every time!

Evening I think Tom is starting to regret coming on this journey. He misses Bruno terribly and does not have a scientific purpose to sustain him as I do. I must go and look for that little Othnielia. A dinosaur pet would undoubtedly cheer him up.

A visit from this inquisitive dinosaur would cheer Tom up no end.

Othnielia

Amphicoelias droppings.

Personal note: The Amphicoelias is Father's favourite dinosaur. He exchanged many letters about it with Edward Drinker Cope, the American scientist who found the first bone in 1877. If I could just see and record one of these gigantic creatures, it would be a dream come true.

Peggy the Steggy
Day 9 in the Jurassic Period

Tom and i had a perfect view of the creature.

Midday I have spent the last few days bringing all the entries in my journal up to date and finishing off the sketches and colour paintings. Part of me is very pleased with this work, but another part of me is saying, 'Why bother? Who is going to look at all this stuff in my journal?'

Sunset Feeling tired from my exertions, I slept with some big ferns covering me, while Tom went exploring on his own. I was rudely awakened when Tom came rushing back to say that there was a dinosaur that I really must see!

It was a Stegosaurus! This has been my favourite dinosaur since I was a little girl. Father used to make up bedtime stories about one named Peggy. When he called her 'Peggy the Steggy,' I used to chuckle and clap my hands!

This harmless plant eater, bristling with body armour, spent ages drinking from a nearby stream. Tom and I had a perfect view of the creature and I was able to make detailed observations and sketches of it.

The Stegosaurus walks with its back arched and its head close to the ground.

The distinctive footprint of my favourite dinosaur.

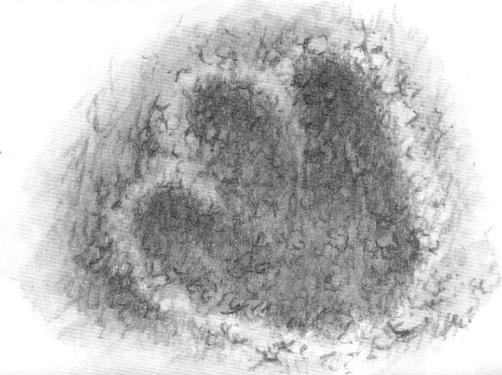

Stegosaurus (pronounced 'Steg-oh-saw-rus' meaning 'roof lizard) was about 9 metres long and 4 metres tall. That is about the size of the motor omnibus that stops in the village and takes people into town twice a week.

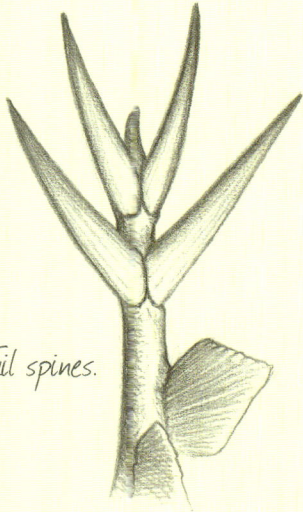

These tail spines are definitely for defence. The animal keeps its tail horizontal as it walks along, so it can swing from left to right. A blow from one of these sword-like spikes would be extremely painful – or fatal!

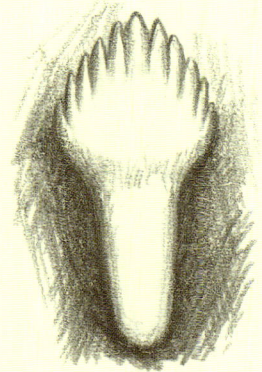

Tail spines.

Stegosaurus have teeth designed to shear off vegetation. The food is then swallowed without chewing.

Specialised tooth.

I used to think that these plates and spikes sticking out of its body were simply for defence, but Father's notes point out that they also helped to control the animal's body temperature.

The savage Allosaurus attack that Tom and I witnessed earlier today.

Diplodocus

Allosaurus are formidable when they hunt on their own. As a pack of three they looked unstoppable.

A devastating bite to the leg enabled the Allosaurus to bring down their giant quarry.

Allosaurus Attack!

Day 10 in the Jurassic Period

The ferocity of the attack sickened me.

Midday Tom and I woke this morning to find that our camp was in the midst of a passing herd of Diplodocus. Fearing that we may be squashed by the gigantic sauropods, we swiftly abandoned camp and scrambled up a nearby rocky precipice. From our raised viewing position we watched the Diplodocus herd feeding for over an hour.

The tranquillity was shattered by the appearance of three large Allosaurus. They had noticed that an ailing member of the herd had become slightly detached from the group. Unperturbed by the threat of the Diplodocus' thrashing tail, one of the predators grabbed its leg, severing the tendons and sending it crashing to the ground. The other Allosaurus piled in to help their hunting partner.

The hunt, from the moment the Allosaurus spotted their victim until they felled it, lasted just fifty seconds. Horrifically, the enormous Diplodocus took a further twenty minutes to die.

The Allosaurus jostled for position, as they chewed through the tough hide and clamped their jaws around the victim's neck in an attempt to stop it breathing. The sound of the Diplodocus gargling and wheezing made my blood run cold, and the three Allosaurus provided a chilling accompaniment of contented grunts and growls.

When they could feast no more they pulled away, their faces covered in blood. They quickly moved on to catch-up with the herd, no doubt to pick out their next unfortunate target.

Anatomy of a Kill

Day 10 in the Jurassic Period

I seized the chance to improve my knowledge of dinosaur anatomy.

Late Afternoon

What was left of the Diplodocus' body lay on the ground, gnawed and bleeding. Tom was disgusted and went straight back to camp. I felt sickened … until my scientific attitude took over and I realised this was a chance to improve my knowledge of dinosaur anatomy and further my drawing and painting skills. So here is my special study of a dead Diplodocus that I have entitled: Anatomy of a Kill.

Name: Diplodocus (pronounced 'Dip-plod-oh-cus' and meaning 'double beam').
Field notes and observations: Belongs with the other plant-eating dinosaurs that I recorded at the beginning of this Jurassic expedition. Of all the sauropods, Diplodocus is the best known and the most widespread. It has a very long neck and tail, as compared to the size of its body, and a particularly small head. I estimate that the specimen I observed was in the region of thirty metres in length.

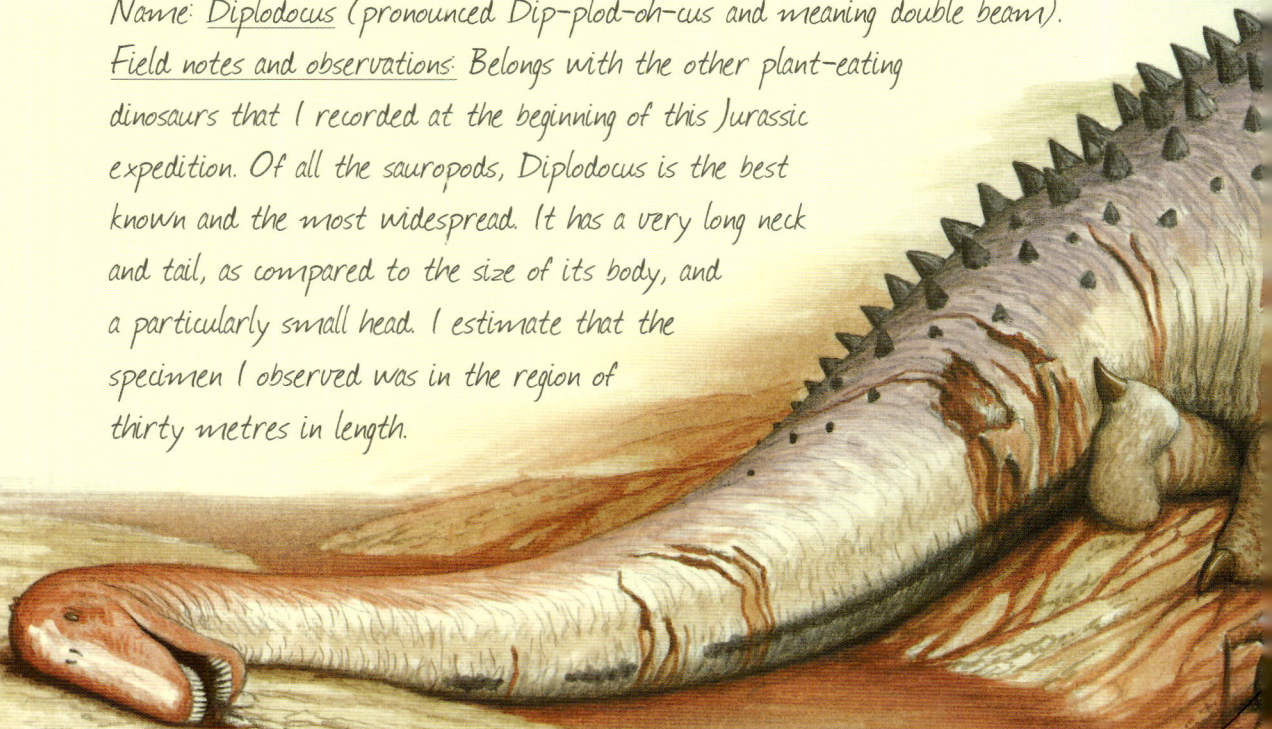

Anatomy of a Kill

Heart

Diplodocus gains its reputation for being stupid from the fact that its brain cavity is so small in relation to its overall size. Even Father seems to agree with this notion, but I would like to challenge it. How intelligent do you need to be to wander around munching leaves all day? In my opinion, all of the species in this group had just the right amount of brainpower for their lifestyle.

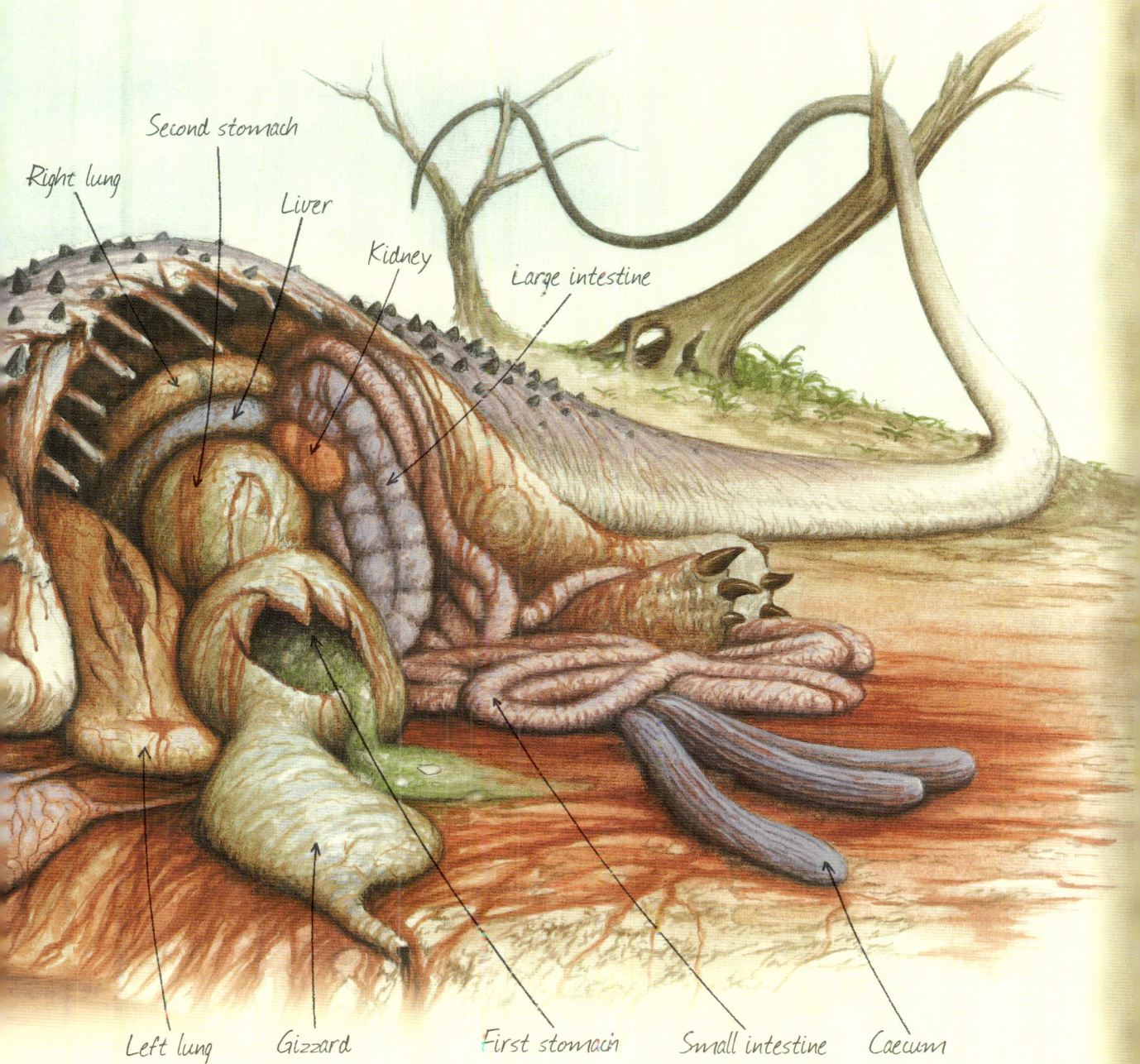

Second stomach

Right lung

Liver

Kidney

Large intestine

Left lung   Gizzard   First stomach   Small intestine   Caecum

What is the group name for Archaeopteryx?

Beasts in Flight

Day 11 in the Jurassic Period

Tom and I spent an enjoyable afternoon observing the flying reptiles.

Today's sighting has made this whole trip worthwhile. Lots of Archaeopteryx have just passed over our heads (we had previously observed only a few of these impressive creatures).

We were gathering our things together, preparing to go home, when I noticed a dark shape approaching in the sky. Looking up, I would have sworn that a noisy flock of crows (correction, a murder of crows) was gliding past. They were about the same size and shape as the modern birds, but were, in fact, small meat-eating reptiles covered with feathers!

Having dropped everything that we were doing, I grabbed my sketch pad and pencil and we raced after the flock. Our luck was in! They chose to roost on a big bush level with a fern-covered outcrop of rock. From this perfect 'hide', Tom and I were able to observe the animals, at first hand, for the whole afternoon.

As a result, I made numerous detailed field notes and observations, which have allowed me to produce this splendid entry in my journal. Even Tom admired my paintings. Usually, he just grunts and says 'They're all right.'

I risked being out after nightfall to claim this most valuable of treasures – an Archaeopteryx feather.

An Archaeopteryx in flight.

Here is my sketch of the flying reptile's wing (below). I am not sure these wings work as well as those of a modern bird. I never saw any of the Archaeopteryx flapping them and taking off. They seemed content to launch themselves from high places and glide for long distances.

Archaeopteryx (pronounced 'Ark-ee-op-ter-ix', meaning 'first bird').

The Archaeopteryx that I saw were about half a metre long. They had wide, rounded wings and a long tail. They were not pretty in the way many modern birds are pretty, but they were not unattractive either.

Father's hero, the naturalist Charles Darwin, was interested in Archaeopteryx. In his famous book 'The Origin of Species', he argues that modern birds evolved from flying lizards. This creature seems to prove his case.

A Happy Afternoon

Day 12 in the Jurassic Period

The ground shook for several minutes ... it felt like an earthquake.

10.30am Would you believe it! Just as we were about to leave, that little Othnielia came back and wanted to be friendly. I thought that he must be very hungry. I gave him some food (not that I had much left) and he gobbled it up. Then he pestered me for more. He is a harmless-looking little thing. It is such a shame this did not happen earlier. He would have made a perfect playmate for Tom.

12.01pm The ground shook for several minutes just now. It felt like an earthquake. Or was it a herd of gigantic dinosaurs passing nearby? Amphicoelias, perhaps?

Early Evening I tried to restrain my curiosity, but it was no use. I had to find out if it was the dinosaur I most wanted to see. So I left Tom finishing the packing and rushed down a long leaf-covered slope from the plateau to the valley floor.

I found myself in the strangest of forests! The tree trunks were a peculiar colour, more grey than brown, and they were massive! Also, no light came filtering down from above. It was silent and gloomy and I did not like it at all. And then … one of the tree trunks moved!

With my heart beating wildly in my chest, I realised what was going on. I was not in a forest at all. I was underneath a herd of sauropod dinosaurs. Were they Amphicoelias? Yes, they were! I started to dash back to the time machine to tell Tom and fetch my art things, but then I slowed down. There was no hurry. These creatures were not going anywhere fast!

Back at camp, I found the little Othnielia and three of his friends pestering Tom for food. I was so keen to get on with my mission, I told him to give them the last of our supplies and come with me.

Tom and I spent one of the happiest afternoons of our lives in the giants' company. The Amphicoelias found themselves a feeding ground of lush vegetation close by, so they were within touching distance. Tom gazed at them in wonder, his jaw dropping at their truly awesome size. I was more practical, sketching and painting them as fast as I could. They are enormous! No wonder Father is so excited by this species. They are the most breathtaking sight I have ever seen!

Name: Amphicoelias (pronounced 'Am-fee-seel-ee-us' and meaning 'double cavities').

A Daring Rescue

August 25th, 1915

I thought that my brother and I would come to a tragic end.

I could not sleep, not because I was excited at the prospect of going home, but because of the Othnielia. He had been joined by a whole host of his fellows, all starving hungry, and I had nothing to give them. We carried our bedding into the time machine and lifted our tent. They fed on the insects squirming underneath.

As I closed the door to the time machine, in preparation for take-off, I realised that I did not have my journal with me. It was outside. I had put it down on a rock when we moved our tent, so I went out to fetch it – and promptly found myself set upon by hordes of pecking Othnielia! One of these creatures on its own was harmless enough, but several dozen of them, all together, was quite a different matter. They were demanding and aggressive and threatened to overwhelm me by their sheer weight of numbers.

With scratched and bleeding legs, I managed to reach my journal – but when I tried to return, my way was blocked by a whole sea of irate, snapping dinosaurs. Seeing my plight, Tom burst out of the time machine and tried to rescue me, but they turned on him as well. Now both of us were trapped! The Othnielia were making a horrible, threatening noise, and I thought that my brother and I would come to a tragic end … until I heard a familiar barking sound in the distance.

Bruno raced up and scattered the Othnielia in all directions. He was still alive and had come back to rescue us!

It all moved very fast after that. Tom bundled the dog into the cabin, thinking the blood on his hands was his own, while I set the dial for home. For one agonising minute, the time machine did not respond. Then it lifted off and we soon found ourselves back in the shed with the summer house clock showing the exact time and date on which we had departed.

Poor Bruno. He has been badly injured by the Othnielia who scratched and pecked him viciously as he dispersed them. Tom and I took him straight to Mr Hutchins, our kindly local vet, who patched him up and said he would soon recover. 'Has he been fighting with a pack of wild dogs?' he asked. 'No, a pack of angry little dinosaurs,' replied Tom without thinking. Mr Hutchins looked at us both and laughed until the tears ran down his face, soaking his bushy, black beard.

Bruno scattered
the Othnielia.

WHAT A DAY! I'm suddenly very tired and cannot wait for a good night's sleep in my cosy WARM bed! It's good to be home.

Reptiles of the Jurassic Period

A comparative scale study

Following the success of my previous scale study, I have attempted the same feat to mark the end of my Jurassic adventure. It still doesn't seem possible that I have observed all of these creatures in the flesh!

Important note:
m = metres and cm = centimetres.

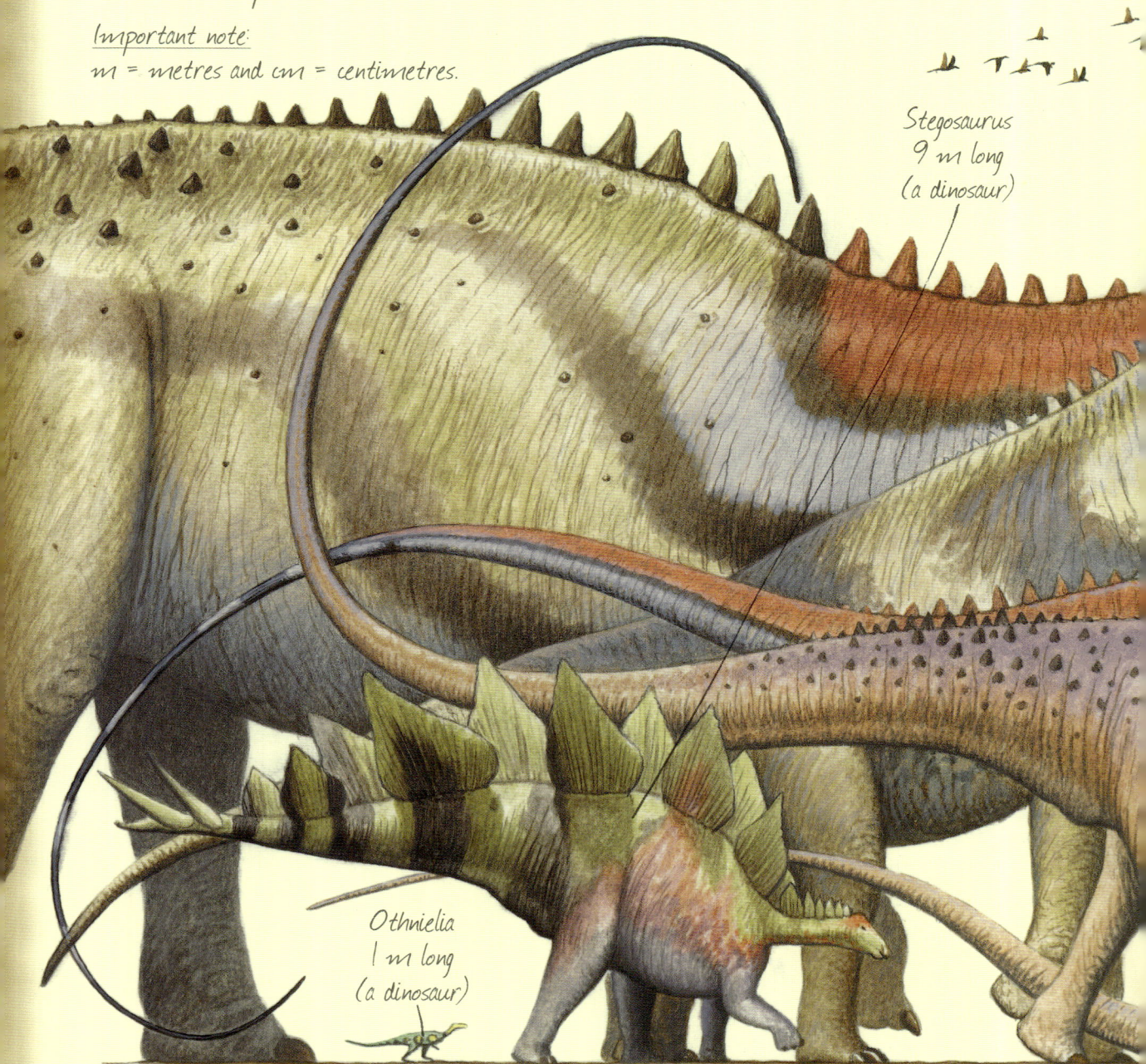

Stegosaurus
9 m long
(a dinosaur)

Othnielia
1 m long
(a dinosaur)

Sordes
60 cm wingspan
(a pterosaur)

Amphicoelias
60 m long
(a dinosaur)

Brachiosaurus
25 m long
(a dinosaur)

Archaeopteryx
80 cm wingspan
(a dinosaur)

Barosaurus
27 m long
(a dinosaur)

Apatosaurus
30 m long
(a dinosaur)

Diplodocus
33 m long
(a dinosaur)

Allosaurus
12 m long
(a dinosaur)

Dryosaurus
3 m long
(a dinosaur)

A Dreadful Week

September 1st, 1915

There is a third age of dinosaurs that I have not yet visited.

Ogh! What a week! Mama decided that I was run down and needed a change of scenery. So, I have been away to the seaside for a week … with Cousin Millicent and Aunt Harriet! I dared not risk taking this journal away with me for fear that it would be stolen and its secrets revealed.

While we're on the subject of secrets, that wretched Mr Givens must have told Mama about my recent purchases. She questioned me about them over breakfast this morning. I must confess, I lied dreadfully to conceal the truth. I said that all the camping equipment and supplies were a gift for the new Scouting movement. I explained that I was a great believer in the health benefits of the great outdoors, but I did not want anyone to know about my charitable act and so kept quiet about it. Mama was quite satisfied with this. As a vicar's wife, she sees it as her role to help the poor.

Note to Self: Must buy new supplies in town. Don't forget to purchase an emergency flare!

One good thing has come out of this dreadful week. I have resolved to go time-travelling with Tom again. According to Father's book, there is a third age of dinosaurs that I have not yet visited. It is called the Cretaceous Period and it finished very abruptly 65 MYA. Maybe I can find out why?

One final reflection on my trip to the seaside … As I stood on the beach, looking out to sea, I thought that just over the horizon men like my Father are fighting a war. Yet here we are, going about our business as if nothing is happening. I feel really upset whenever I think about it …

My Journey To
THE CRETACEOUS PERIOD

The Cretaceous Period was
144-65 Million Years Ago

Triceratops Sightings
Day 1 in the Cretaceous Period

65 million years ago.

We arrived safely in the late Cretaceous Period, 65 million years ago. We left at 6 am and the journey took over two hours. This is longer than ever before. The crystal is definitely malfunctioning! I did not say anything to Tom, but I am very anxious about getting home.

Side profile of a muscular Triceratops.

Our first sighting was a Triceratops. There is no mistaking this dinosaur, with three huge horns sticking out of its head and that colourful bony frill around its neck. The latter looks like a ruff worn by an Elizabethan gentleman. I expect we shall see a lot more of these stocky plant eaters. They live in big herds, I believe.

Triceratops (pronounced 'Try-serra-tops', meaning 'three-horned face').

Field notes and observations: The Triceratops lives in great herds and can be easily identified by its large skull, colourful neck frill and the three horns that protrude from its face. It is in the region of nine metres long.

The herd hierarchy appears to be determined by sparring and a locking of head shields with the weaker combatant yielding prior to serious injury taking place. I have yet to witness the prominent horns being used in these jousts. Father's book mentions that they may be used as a means of defence against Tyrannosaurs and other large predators.

The skull, including the neck frill, is over two metres long and is used as a defensive shield.

'The Prof'

Day 3 in the Cretaceous Period

These strange-looking creatures are very distinctive.

So far, my visit to the Cretaceous has been very rewarding. Yesterday, I saw a well-known duck-billed dinosaur. Today, I saw a different one. The scientific name for this group is 'hadrosaur'. Both are very paintable. That is why these pages are given over to portraits and notes about these two herbivorous creatures.

Looking at my finished picture of the Parasaurolophus, it reminds me of an ancient Egyptian carving of a Pharaoh.

Note to Self:
Ancient Egypt would be a fascinating place to visit in my time machine!

An adult, 13-metre-long
Parasaurolophus.

Field notes:
Pronounced 'Pah-rah-saw-roll-off-us' and meaning 'near crested lizard,' this strange-looking creature is even more distinctive than Triceratops thanks to the enormous bony crest that sticks out from the back of its head. This crest is two metres long. According to Father's notes, it was used for communication between the animals and for display by the males.

The second hadrosaur that I observed was even stranger than 'Pharaoh'. This one reminded me of a professor with lots of brains in a big, domed head, so my nickname for him is 'The Prof.'

The other special feature of this dinosaur is the long line of spines down its back. They are very short and reach right down to its tail. They look like a very tiny Great Wall of China!

'The Prof' reared up on his strong back legs to eat the leaves from some bushes. We followed him as he wandered away on all fours. Then, as we saw the creature tending to some eggs on a nesting site nearby, Tom chuckled: 'Look, Netty – "he" is a "she"!' One of the eggs hatched out as we watched, and a miniature Hypacrosaurus struggled into the world. It was so sweet!

Hypacrosaurus (pronounced 'High-pah-kroe-sore-uss' and meaning 'near top lizard').

Field notes and observations: The Hypacrosaurus is in the region of twelve metres in length It has a toothless bill, followed by rows of teeth located in its cheeks. The tail of Hypacrosaurus is very long and stiff and appears to be used as a weight to balance the animal as it moves. Like many other duck-bills, Hypacrosaurus has a prominent crest located on the top of its head. The melon-sized eggs that Tom and I saw were laid in rows and were covered with earth and plant material.

Hypacrosaurus

Uninvited Creature

Day 4 in the Cretaceous Period

A visit from a friendly creature livened up a dull day.

A small, bird-like dinosaur has started following Tom around as he goes about his daily business. I told my brother to completely ignore the creature. After the dreadful ordeal with the Othnielia on our last journey, we want no interaction with it at all.

We have tried to shoo this animal away on numerous occasions today. It refuses to take no for an answer! The creature is obviously very intelligent. Just now, we watched it using a stone as a tool to crack open an egg.

Troodon (pronounced 'Trow-oh-don' and meaning 'wounding tooth'). Observations: I would guess it is about two metres long and one metre tall. It runs very fast and reminds me of a small ostrich. It appears to have a thumb just like ours, which enables it to grip things in its claws.

He is so friendly! What can we call him? It will have to be 'Fred' for the moment. A suitable name will no doubt occur.

Troodon (Fred)

Galahad

Day 5 in the Cretaceous Period

Fred is now called Galahad, the bravest of King Arthur's knights.

Earlier today Fred rushed into our campsite, squawked at me, pecked Tom on the ankle and ran off. Then he waited at the foot of some nearby rocks, clucking impatiently. We would have needed to be very stupid not to understand that he wanted us to follow him, so we did. We scrambled up a steep hill until we reached a flat area at the top of a big rock.

At first, nothing happened. Then I realised he had saved our lives! Suddenly, below us, a massive Tyrannosaurus burst out of the tall ferns and strode through the camp, flattening the tent beneath its huge feet. Then the beast looked all around, gave a terrifying roar and marched on.

Field notes:
The name says it all –
Tyrannosaurus, pronounced
'Tie-ran-oh-saw-rus' and
meaning 'tyrant lizard'. The one
that rampaged through camp
today was about 5 metres tall
and 12 metres long. I could not
tell if it was male or female –
both must be equally terrifying!
It has no natural predators and
literally rules the Earth!

Tyrannosaurus rex

Pachycephalosaurs
Day 6 in the Cretaceous Period

How did Father know so much about dinosaurs?

Mid-morning Tom has a terrible cold! One moment he is burning hot, the next moment he is shivering and shaking like a jelly. I want to take him home, but he will not hear of it. He says he just wants to lie quietly in the tent until the fever passes.

Afternoon Several herds of very unusual dinosaurs are passing by on the plains. I must study them. I looked up the species in Father's book and discovered that they are pachycephalosaurs. I did not know what that meant – until I found an explanation beside his notes. Not only do I think Father intended me to use his time machine, he knew I would visit the age of the dinosaurs and expected me to take his book as well!

A pachycephalosaur

Pachycephalosaur
(pronounced 'Pack-ee-seff-allo-saw' and meaning 'thick-headed lizard').
Observations: The dinosaurs in this group have thick, bony skulls. They have short spikes sticking out on either side of the bony dome covering the top of the head and more spikes sticking up from the snout.

IMPORTANT NOTE:
How did Father know so much about dinosaurs? Did he use the time machine to visit the FUTURE to gain the knowledge on which I now rely?

This species is called Stegoceras
(pronounced 'Steg-oss-er-ass' and meaning 'horned roof').
I expected to see the males using their large heads to
butt one another and decide the strongest male (like
rutting stags), but this did not happen.
Perhaps they use them for some other purpose?

Stegoceras

I noticed a further dinosaur lying on the ground. This one
looked different from the other two and was injured or sick.

A Brave Fight
Day 7 in the Cretaceous Period

'All day long, the noise of battle rolled' – Alfred Tennyson.

All night, I could not stop thinking about the third species that I observed yesterday. The poor thing is in such danger, lying out in the open all on its own. I felt that I must go and see if it was all right.

Tom said I was being ridiculous. How could I possibly help a five-metre-long dinosaur with a head like a tombstone covered in spikes?

Leaving Tom still protesting, I returned to the scene … and found that the stricken creature was not there. Then I heard a terrible commotion. Looking across the plain in the opposite direction, I saw my stricken creature struggling along while being attacked by three smallish carnivores. Without Father's book, I could not tell what they were.

I have identified the third species of pachycephalosaur as a Stygimoloch (pronounced 'Sty-gimm-oh-lock' and meaning 'horned devil from the river of death').

The brave fight!

74

'All day long, the noise of battle rolled,' as my dear Tennyson said in his 'Idylls of the King'. This brave Stygimoloch was not going to give up without a fight Time after time, the pack of predators attacked him – and on each occasion, he repelled them. He used his heavy, bony head with its ring of spikes to butt them in the stomach. In the end, they gave up and slunk away while my hero limped off to find his fellow beasts.

Not only have I witnessed and recorded a life-and-death prehistoric conflict, I have also established the function of the bony heads of these dinosaurs. They are used for self-defence by targeting vulnerable parts of a predator.

Name: Dromœosaurus (pronounced 'Dro-mee-o-sawr-us' and meaning fast-running lizard).

Field notes and observations: The three fierce specimens that I observed were agile creatures with a large sickle-shaped killing claw on each back foot. They worked together in an attempt to bring down the Stygimoloch and are obviously very intelligent.

Detailed head of a Dromœosaurus.

The lucky Stygimoloch

Reptile Attack!

Day 8 in the Cretaceous Period

A shock encounter with the largest flying reptile of all time!

Tom awoke this morning feeling a lot better. He still gives the occasional loud sneeze, but his fever has passed. He told me to go a bit further afield, to observe some different terrain, while he got his strength back. He would accompany me on my next expedition.

A well-worn dinosaur trail led me down towards some marshy wetlands near to the coast. Galahad followed just behind me, clucking like an anxious mother hen. The atmosphere grew increasingly tropical as we approached some big lagoons, so I imagined my little friend was complaining about the heat. How wrong I was!

Suddenly, out of the clear blue sky, the biggest flying reptile I have ever seen swooped down towards us. Galahad pushed me into some reeds, preventing the creature from gripping me in its talons. To my horror, it returned and picked up Galahad!

Detailed study of Quetzalcoatlus head and beak.

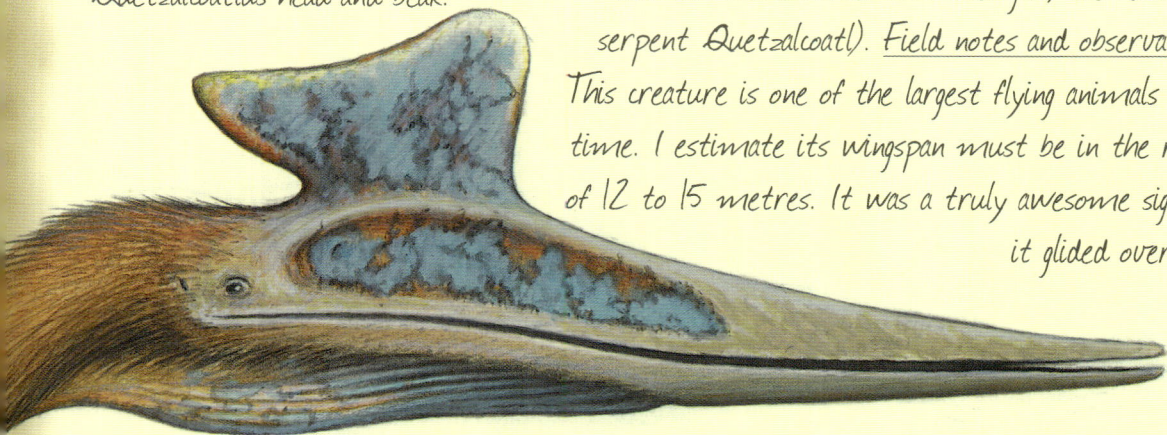

Name: Quetzalcoatlus (pronounced 'Quet-zall-coat-luss' and named after an Aztec god, the feathered serpent Quetzalcoatl). Field notes and observations: This creature is one of the largest flying animals of all time. I estimate its wingspan must be in the region of 12 to 15 metres. It was a truly awesome sight as it glided overhead.

I watched aghast as the monster carried him upwards, struggling and shrieking. What could I do? Nothing! I felt so helpless and angry … until I remembered the flare I had bought!

I snatched the flare out of my rucksack and set it off, making a loud BANG and sending a column of searing red light into the air. This startled the giant reptile, causing it to drop poor Galahad, who fell harmlessly into some shallow water nearby. I pulled him out and we hurried back to Tom like a couple of naughty children who had just got away with a clever prank!

Quetzalcoatlus used its giant wings to ride thermals for hundreds of miles.

Note: Father's book says that the Quetzalcoatlus has very keen eyesight and, like modern birds of prey, can spot its food at long range. Its long neck and toothless jaws make it perfectly adapted to feeding on carrion, while its long talons suggest that it may also hunt for fish.

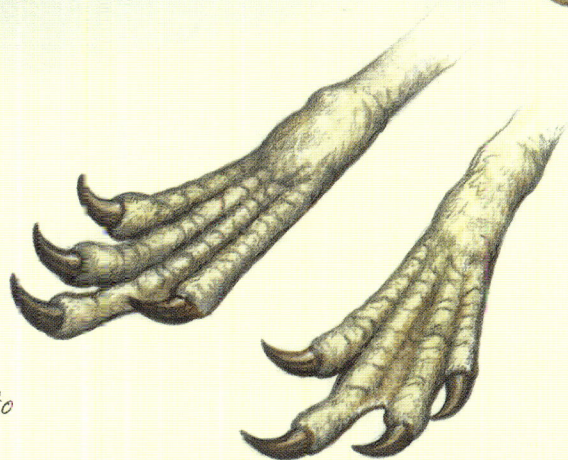

Quetzalcoatlus talons.

Face from Hell
Day 9 in the Cretaceous Period

This time it was Tom's turn to act foolishly.

Last night a new star appeared in the night sky. It was much brighter than any of the other stars around it. It looked very beautiful. As I sat, gazing up at its dazzling light, Galahad came over and rested his head on my knee. It was a magical moment.

Tom was fine after another good night's sleep, so we both went to explore some woodland in search of other herbivore dinosaurs. Galahad, as usual, came tagging along behind. Yet this little expedition triggered a sequence of terrible events from which we have not yet recovered.

Maybe writing it all down in this journal will help me come to terms with what has happened. Then perhaps I can be of comfort to my brother.

There were no plant-eating dinosaurs in these woods. This seemed strange because there was an abundance of food all around. The reason soon became clear. Right in the middle of the woodland was a large T-rex nest.

Last night a bright new star appeared in the night sky.

The trapped baby T-rex.

This time, it was Tom's turn to act foolishly. Despite my repeated warnings and Galahad's shrieks of protest, Tom sneaked over to the nest and collected a sliver of shell from a broken egg. He wanted it as a souvenir. It got lost in the ensuing nightmare.

We were about to return to camp when we heard a loud squealing noise coming from a thick copse close behind us. It sounded like an animal in trouble and I wanted to investigate, but Galahad would not let me. He pecked me really hard to prevent me going any closer. Fool that I am, this only made me more determined to know what was wrong, so I pushed him roughly aside and strode into the copse.

In the clearing, I found a baby T-rex with its tail caught by a fallen branch. It was trapped, and its cries of pain and frustration were heart-rending. With Galahad squawking at me like a mad turkey, I told Tom to help me shift the heavy branch. It was almost beyond our strength, but somehow we managed to lift it sufficiently for the little Tyrannosaurus to struggle free.

Then we both looked up and found ourselves staring into a face from hell!

– account continued on next page

– continued from previous page

It was the mother T-rex! She had arrived in response to her infant's distress cries – and thought we were responsible for causing them! She bellowed at us in fury.

For once in my life, I did not panic. 'Keep perfectly still,' I whispered to Tom. 'Don't move a muscle or utter a sound.' So we stood there, like a pair of petrified statues, with the monster sniffing all around us. I thought our plan was going to work because the killer started to move away from us. Then Tom gave one of his explosive sneezes! The T-rex rounded on us in a flash. Grandmama had always said that colds could be life-threatening – but I don't think she imagined anything like this!

Everything happened in a blur after that. I saw the ghastly creature open her enormous jaws, ready to eat us both alive. I closed my eyes, steeling myself against the searing pain. But it did not happen! Instead, Galahad threw himself forward and pushed the two of us out of the way. Then I saw his little form being picked up in the killer's mouth, pumping blood in all directions as he was bitten in half.

The brief diversion allowed us to make our escape. Tom and I ran faster than we ever thought possible, dashing through the thin trees with the bellowing T-rex thundering after us. As we ran, I vowed to go home at the first opportunity … if it arose!

Suddenly, the adult T-rex called off the chase and left us alone. Maybe her baby was calling again or she spotted some other prey. Whatever the reason, we charged into camp and leapt into the time machine, slamming and locking the door behind us. Then we clung onto each other, alternately trembling with shock and weeping at the heroic sacrifice of our brave little dinosaur friend.

Tyrannosaurus rex –
the face from hell!

The dagger–like teeth that tore into
Galahad were 15 cm in length.

Field notes and observations:

The Tyrannosaurus rex is the largest known terrestrial carnivore. According to
Father's notes, an adult was in the region of twelve metres long, six metres tall
and could weigh more than seven tonnes. Although Tom and I attempted to fool
the beast by remaining still, the notes reveal that T-rex had exceptional eyesight
and a powerful sense of smell. If this is true, I can only assume that this
fearsome predator was distracted by our strange human odour and not by our
foolhardy attempt to remain motionless. Based on my first meeting with this
species, I can confirm the entry that states 'the T-rex was, most likely, an
ambush predator'.

Special note: Telling the story has helped me to cope with my ordeal. I have
painted this picture of my mighty assailant in the hope it will sponge away this
horrible episode.

A Slim Hope

Stuck in the Cretaceous Period

Are we stranded here for the rest of our lives?

Day 10 When Tom and I had regained our composure, I set the time dial and pushed the switch. Nothing happened! The green crystal glowed a little and the time machine shook slightly, but failed to lift off. Clearly, it did not have enough power to raise itself off the ground. Today, I cannot help but wonder, 'Are we stranded here for the rest of our lives?'

Day 11 I weep whenever I think about Galahad or our own terrible predicament. I am no help to poor Tom. Quite the opposite. He remains resolutely cheerful and keeps saying, 'Don't worry, sis, something will turn up.' Bless him. Deep down inside, he must be really frightened. No further entries today.

Day 14 Something has occurred which has slightly restored our spirits. During one of the thunderstorms, which happen almost daily, a tree close to the time machine was struck by lightning. Watching the enormous power of the lightning, a thought occurred to me. Perhaps the crystal needs an occasional electrical charge to keep it fully active. So maybe if our powerless ship was struck by lightning …

We spent the afternoon clearing vegetation and foliage from around the time machine to expose it as fully as possible. I am aware that the odds against a successful strike are millions to one, but at least it gives us a smattering of hope. I pray that my theory is correct!

Maybe it is a wishing star? Here's my wish – I wish we could go home!

Late Evening That star appeared again tonight. It looked ten times brighter and very much larger than before. I could have sworn it was moving. Anyone would think it was falling out of the sky!

Day 15 Tom and I agreed to continue searching for new dinosaur species to take our minds off our troubles and pass the time. Our renewed determination was rewarded by a sighting of a very interesting plant-eating dinosaur.

Name: Ankylosaurus (pronounced 'An-kile-oh-saw-rus' and meaning 'stiff lizard').
Field notes and observations: A plant eater with lots of special features to ward off attacks by carnivorous predators.

An armour-plated back.

Four pointed growths on its head: one above and behind each eye and one below each eye.

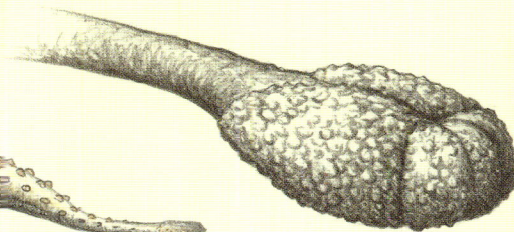

A bony tail that can be swung to and fro like a club.

Father's book says that the bones of this creature were first found recently, in 1908, by his great friend, Barnum Brown. What a colourful character Father's friend is! He always wears a tie, a jacket and a full-length fur coat when he goes hunting for dinosaur fossils!

Impending Doom
Day 16 in the Cretaceous Period

Tom and I feel unbearably lonely and homesick.

Morning Just as we were beginning to recover our composure, we heard it again – the hideous bellowing of the Tyrannosaurus rex! Neither of us can face another encounter with this terrible creature, so we are moving to higher ground to make absolutely sure we keep out of danger.

3.30pm The view from our new camp is magnificent. After falling asleep, I woke up to see a strange-looking ceratopcian wandering past

Name: <u>Leptoceratops</u>
Pronunciation: 'Leapt-oh-serra-tops'
Meaning of name: 'Lean-horned face'
Habitat: Southern states of North America
Diet: Ferns, cycads and conifers. Size: About 2 metres
Weight: Anywhere between 50 to 150 kilograms
Notes: It walks on all four legs, but can stand on its back legs and reach up for food. It has five clawed fingers on each hand. Its mouth is shaped like that of a modern-day parrot.

just below us. I spent two hours sketching and painting the creature, who kept reasonably still as it gnawed its way through a bank of lush green ferns, biting them off one by one with its sharp, parrot-like bill.

Evening The world is bathed in an eerie light from that strange star. It has grown even bigger than before and now shines like the moon. Even the dinosaurs appear to have noticed it. Tom and I watched a whole herd of Triceratops wander into the valley below. They appeared nervous. Perhaps it is this strange light, but it feels as if something terrible is about to happen.

The strange star bathes the day in a most peculiar light.

Dinosaurs are fascinating creatures, but they live in a world even more dangerous and violent than our own.

In Cold Blood

Day 17 in the Cretaceous Period

We watched the conflict in all its gory detail.

Sunset We awoke from a fitful sleep to the sound of roaring and bellowing from the plain below. No wonder the herd of Triceratops looked nervous last night – they were being stalked by predators! A battle between the armour-plated herbivores and the fast-moving carnivores was in full swing … and my brother and I had a grandstand view!

We watched the conflict in all its gory detail. The Triceratops defended themselves well, but the Tyrannosaurus rex and Nanotyrannus had the advantage of speed – plus an innate urge to kill driven by hunger.

There is no mistaking the ferocious visage of a T-rex, but the smaller predators were far more difficult to identify. I believe them to be Nanotyrannus, pronounced 'Nann-oh-tie-ran-us' and meaning 'tiny tyrant'. It is a good name for them!

Nanotyrannus

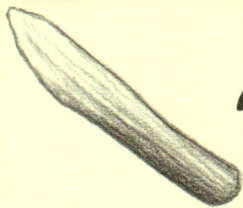

A Dramatic Return

September 2nd, 1915

A miraculous sequence of events.

A peg-shaped tooth from an Alamosaurus.

We are back safely in our own time! Five days have passed since the last entry in my journal. During that period, Tom and I returned from the Cretaceous Period in the most dramatic way imaginable. In fact, it is a miraculous sequence of events that, from the tranquil safety of my beloved summer house, I can now chronicle in full …

Day 18   The strange star now filled the sky like a second moon. It gave me a terrible sense of foreboding. It felt as if the end of the world was nigh.

Day 19   A large herbivorous dinosaur passed by our camp and paused to swallow some leaves from a young cottonwood tree. Its size and shape reminded me of the big sauropod dinosaurs that I saw in the Jurassic Period. I sketched it quickly, vowing to look up the creature when I had more time. In fact, I had plenty of time. It was that weird star that made me feel as if everything had to be done in a hurry.

Day 20 It dawned on me that the star was in fact a meteor – and a big one at that – hurtling towards Earth at breakneck speed. Father had told me about the worldwide devastation these can cause. Realising we were in mortal danger, I rushed back to the time machine and bundled Tom inside. Would the crystal have regenerated? I prayed so with all my heart.

It had not! We tried repeatedly to leave this scene of impending disaster, but on each occasion the time machine struggled and failed to get itself off the ground.

PT.O.

Alamosaurus (pronounced 'Ah-la-mo-saur-russ' and meaning 'Cottonwood lizard'). This creature's peg-shaped teeth were no good for chewing, so foliage was swallowed whole and broken down in the stomach.

Alamosaurus

– continued

Moment of Impact

September 2nd, 1915

The world seemed to be lit like a stage.

Day 21 Kept wondering if, or when, the meteor would hit Earth. Tom kept asking why I was so impatient for it to strike. He argued that until it did, we would remain alive! He can be very wise in a crisis, my little brother.

Day 22 Tom and I remained in the camp all day. Decided to spend the night in prayer, like medieval knights holding a vigil before a great battle the next day. Lasted about twenty minutes. Both fell asleep.

The terrible moment arrived while we were still asleep! Tom and I were woken by a blinding white light, followed swiftly by an unbearable heat. Seconds later, we were thrown into the air like puppets.

The super-heated blast, caused by the impact of the meteor, had thrown our time machine high into the air, engulfing us in flames! We were off the ground!

With my heart threatening to burst through my chest I frantically set the dial to 1915 AD and pushed the switch. As the flames seared our time machine, we heard the familiar rushing noise and felt the wonderful sensation of the machine speeding up ready to travel through time. We were making our escape! We were saved!

As we departed, I looked through the porthole window for one last glimpse at the prehistoric world. What I saw will be etched on my mind for the rest of my days. It was a scene of utter devastation, far worse than anything Father had ever envisaged. I cannot begin to describe all that I saw in that one brief moment.

Once again, the summer house clock resumed ticking as Tom and I emerged from the scorched time machine. Nobody knows where we have been, what we have done and how close we have both been to death … except you, my dear Journal.

It is harrowing to think that the wonderful creatures I observed during my expedition would have perished in the furnace-like heat.

Explanatory note:
With the diminished power of the crystal, our craft could not get off the ground by itself – but the disaster did the job for us!

My illustration of the apocalyptic impact.

Reptiles of the Cretaceous Period

A comparative scale study

This is the final illustration of my adventures in the time of the dinosaurs.
I hope to share my field notes and observations on this dramatic period in
Earth's history with Father when he returns from the war.

Important note:
m = metres and
cm = centimetres.

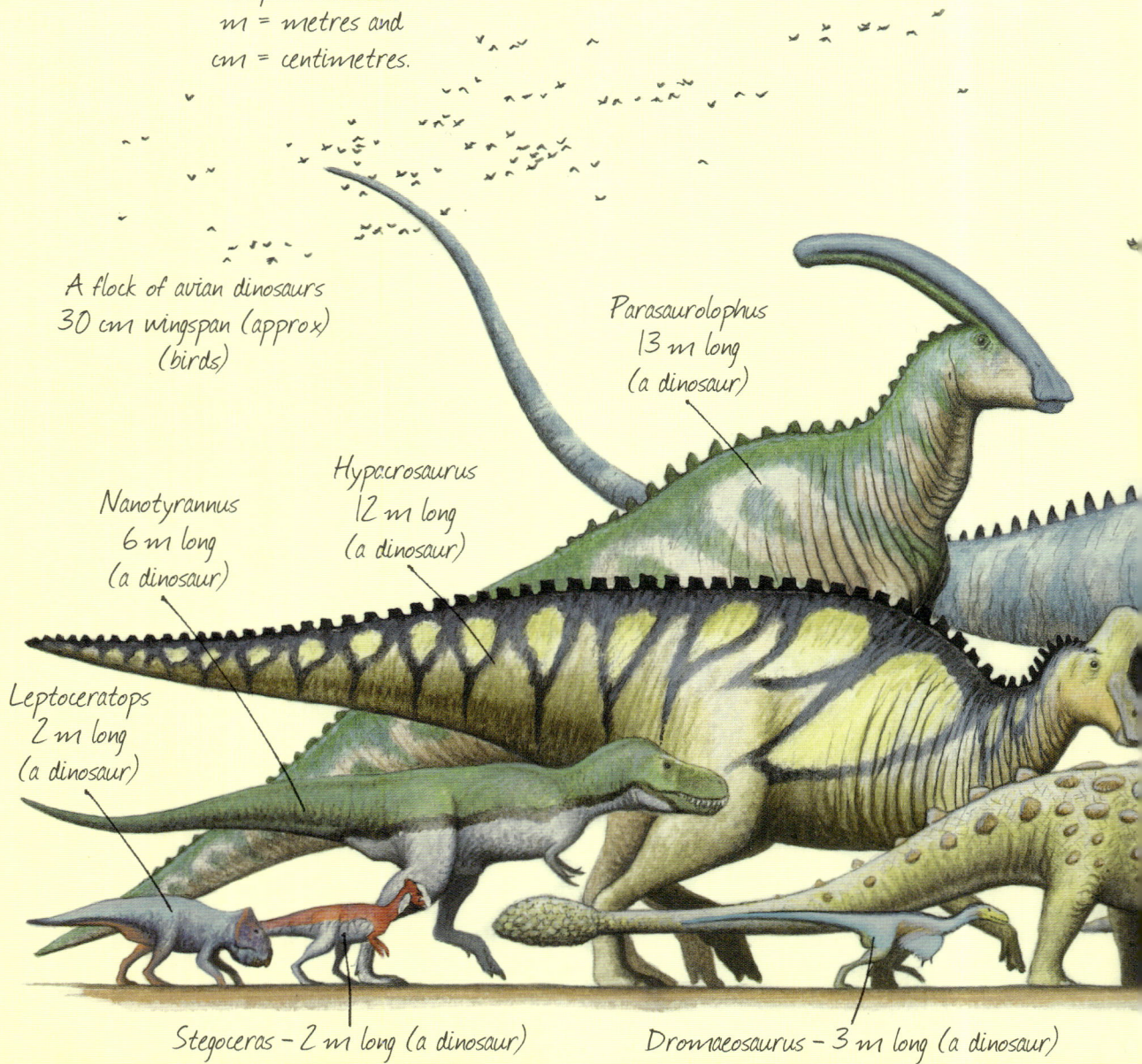

A flock of avian dinosaurs
30 cm wingspan (approx)
(birds)

Parasaurolophus
13 m long
(a dinosaur)

Hypacrosaurus
12 m long
(a dinosaur)

Nanotyrannus
6 m long
(a dinosaur)

Leptoceratops
2 m long
(a dinosaur)

Stegoceras – 2 m long (a dinosaur)

Dromaeosaurus – 3 m long (a dinosaur)

Quetzalcoatlus
14 m wingspan
(a pterosaur)

Aramosaurus
30 m long
(a dinosaur)

Triceratops
9 m long
(a dinosaur)

Tyrannosaurus
12 m long
(a dinosaur)

Pachycephalosaurus
6 m long
(a dinosaur)

Ankylosaurus - 10 m long (a dinosaur)   Stygimoloch - 5 m long (a dinosaur)   Troodon - 2 m long (a dinosaur)

Uncle George
September 3rd, 1915

Banned from the summer house!

Mama was shocked by my appearance as I sat down to luncheon. She said I looked pale and tired and has forbidden me to go anywhere near 'that wretched summer house' for the rest of the summer holidays. I do not mind. Time-travelling is such a worrying and dangerous pastime, I have decided never to do it again.

Afternoon Wonderful news! Uncle George has come to stay! He is Father's twin brother (twins run in our family), but they are not alike. Father is passionate about science and the natural world, George is keen on history. Actually, that is something of an understatement. He is a Professor of History at a big university with a special interest in ancient Egypt.

Uncle George

Tom has promised never to breathe a word of our adventures to anyone. He, like me, wants to recover from his ordeal and is not pestering to go anywhere again. Every now and then, I catch him smiling at me and I know he is relishing our special secret. It has drawn us very close together.

Sep 4th Evening

Earlier today, Uncle George took me to see an exhibition of Egyptian relics. They are on tour. The organiser, Mr Howard Carter, is trying to raise money for a new excavation in the Valley of the Kings. He hopes to find the tomb of the boy-king Tutankhamen, but I doubt if he will succeed where so many others have failed.

i have fallen in love with ancient Egypt! The relics and artefacts on display were so beautiful. No wonder Uncle George is happy to spend his life learning about them.

Aunt Harriet and Cousin Millicent were at this exhibition. They have a motor car! They insisted on giving Uncle George and myself a lift home in it – though, with Aunt Harriet driving, it is a miracle we got home alive. Millicent is very proud of their motor car and insisted on honking the horn at every opportunity. How vulgar can you get?

Sep 5th

I went to the library in town today and borrowed some books on ancient Egypt. They were quite interesting, but lacked any decent illustrations. I would like to see more of this exciting and colourful world. Perhaps I should go there myself …

Goodbye, my Friend
September 6th, 1915

This is where we must part company, dearest Journal.

Yes! That is what I shall do – during the Christmas holidays! I am sure that another term of schoolwork, combined with my tedious home life, will be enough to make me brave the dangers once again. Tom can come with me. It cannot possibly be as hazardous as visiting prehistory, with its savage array of giant bloodthirsty predators.

This is where we must part company, dearest Journal. You are full and I have nothing more to write on the subject of dinosaurs. I shall call you 'A Time-Traveller's Field Notes and Observations of Dinosaurs' to give you a scientific-sounding title, and then hide you away in the summer house for Father or future generations to read. Goodbye, my friend. I shall miss you. You have been such a faithful companion!